I0755752

The Kaiser's Raider!

Kapitänleutnant von Mücke

The Kaiser's Raider!

Two Accounts of the S.M.S. "Emden" During the First World War by One of its Officers

The "Emden"

The "Ayesha" Being the Adventures of the Landing Squad of the "Emden"

Hellmuth von Mücke

Translated by Helene S. White

The Kaiser's Raider!
Two Accounts of the S.M.S. "Emden" During the First World War
by One of its Officers
The "Emden"
and
The "Ayesha" Being the Adventures of the Landing Squad of the "Emden"
by Hellmuth von Mücke

First published under the titles
The "Emden"
and
The "Ayesha" Being the Adventures of the Landing Squad of the "Emden"

FIRST EDITION

Leonaur is an imprint
of Oakpast Ltd

ISBN: 978-0-85706-842-2 (hardcover)
ISBN: 978-0-85706-843 9 (softcover)

http://www.leonaur.com

Publisher's Notes

The views expressed in this book are not necessarily those of the publisher.

Contents

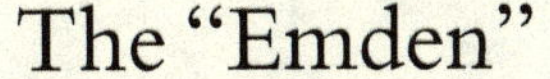

The "Emden"

Contents

Foreword

As Kapitänleutnant von Mücke witnessed the *Emden's* final battle from a distance only, we have no detailed account of the gallant cruiser's last fight. We do know, however, from statements made by survivors, that, owing to a lack of ammunition and the crippling of her steering gear, the *Emden* was finally placed at the mercy of her foe. She was then run aground on the reefs of North Keeling Island at so tremendous a speed that the man at the wheel was instantly killed by the terrific impact. To the enemy's signal, calling for surrender, the customary reply could not be given, as the long continued battle had left but three able-bodied seamen, charged with this duty, to fulfil it. Hereupon the British cruiser fired two more broadsides into the stranded ship.

Finally, at the order of the *Emden's* commander, some of the survivors ran up something white. Before the ship was surrendered, the German flag was torn into shreds and cast into the sea.

More than two years later the English succeeded in salving the *Emden*, and she is now to fight for the enemy she once pursued.

It was from Tsingtao, the charming home port of the German East Asiatic squadron, that the *Emden* sailed forth upon her last cruise. The Germans, regarded this port as the symbol of the open door, and of the equal right of all nations to enter the markets of the far East. In its loss they recognize the fulfilment of the persistent but covert English purpose to deny to Germany all overseas expansion beyond the limit of English tolerance.

Individually and as a nation the Germans have accepted the challenge. As masters of their destiny and as a liberty loving people they are, of course, vastly more interested in the overthrow of England's latent sovereignty of the world than in England's political creed. The object of the German desire is to obtain habitable colonial territory where an overflowing population may live and remain German instead of feeding other nations with German blood. This is pointed out, as otherwise certain passages in the first chapter might seem strangely out of place in this story of heroic adventures.

At the author's request the title he bears as an officer in the Imperial German navy is retained in the translation. In doing his part for his country's defence, he evidently agrees with Goethe:

The riding heroes on solid land
Of greatest moment now may be—
If I but had the full command
On Neptune's horse I'd skim the sea!

Theodor J. Ritter

Boston, Mass.
March, 1917.

Chapter 1

Our First Prize

"All hands aft," shrilled the whistles of the boatswain's mate through all the ship's decks. Quickly all the officers and crew assembled on the after deck. Everyone knew what it was for.

It was at two o'clock on the afternoon of the second day of August, 1914, while our ship lay far out in the Yellow Sea, that Captain von Mueller appeared on the poop, holding in his hand a slip of paper such as is used for messages by wireless. In eager expectancy three hundred pairs of eyes were fixed upon the lips of our commander as he began to speak.

> The following wireless message has just been received from Tsingtao:
>
> > On August first, His Majesty, the Emperor, ordered the mobilization of the entire land and naval forces of the Empire. Russian troops have crossed the border into Germany. As a consequence, the Empire is at war with Russia and with France.
> >
> > And so, what we have expected for years has come about. Before war had been declared, hostile hordes have violated German territory.
> >
> > For forty-four years the German sword has not been drawn from its scabbard, although during this time there has been more than one occasion when it might have been unsheathed for conquest. But never have conquests by violence been the objects of German ambition. In peaceable competition, by diligence and labour, by commercial and industrial efficiency, by high intellectual and educational attainment, by honesty and reliability the

> German people have secured for themselves a place of honour among the nations.
>
> Today the German Empire is an object of envy to those who failed to accomplish as much. Being convinced of their own inability by peaceable methods to compete successfully with the nation that outranks them in learning and education, in technical and scientific skill, in short, by the advanced state of its civilization and its culture, they now hope to accomplish their purpose by letting loose upon the German people the furies of war, and by an appeal to the sword to gain the end they have failed to obtain by moral and intellectual achievement. It now remains for us to show them that the virile German nation can successfully meet this test of its strength also. The victory will be no easy one. For many years our enemies have been preparing for this war. To be, or not to be, that is the question for our nation today. But we shall prove ourselves worthy of our fathers, and of our ancient heritage,—we shall endure to the end, though a world in arms arise against us.

> It is my intention to proceed at once in the direction of Vladivostok. Our first duty is to raid the commerce of the enemy. In so far as can be estimated at present, the French and Russian warships arc assembled in greatest strength in the neighbourhood of Vladivostok. It is therefore probable that we shall encounter them. In that event, I feel confident that I can rely upon my men.

Three cheers for His Majesty, the Emperor, rang out over the broad surface of the Yellow Sea. Then came the order that sent every man to his post,—"Clear ship for action."

And so it had come to pass—the war was upon us! The outcry for revenge that has been incessantly raised to the west of us, and that has been especially clamorous ever since Germany ventured to retake with the sword territory which, since time immemorial, had formed a part of the German Empire, but which, at the time of her impotence and disruption, was wrested from her to gratify French lust for conquest—this persistent cry for revenge had at last achieved its purpose. Again the game of war was to be played, and again the leaden dice were to be cast. But this tune, not merely for the possession of

Elsass-Lothringen,—much more was to be at stake. As yet, only Russia and France were to be faced. But for years it has been evident that behind these two powers stands another, the enemy of all others, one who for centuries has contrived to spill the warm red blood of other races for the purpose of furthering her own interests,—England! Three decades ago, when the French had dared to cross the English plans for colonization in Africa, they were forced to their knees and deeply humiliated at Fashoda. When England had become alarmed at Russia's progress in the far East, that country's defeat at the hands of Japan, in 1904, was brought about.

Ever since these two rivals were thus disposed of, England has directed their attention toward seeking compensation elsewhere for that which English greed for wealth and power denied to them in Asia and in Africa. Humbled France and defeated Russia must be induced to serve England's purpose to annihilate Germany. In the German Empire, strong in the vigour of youth, England recognized her most dangerous rival. By peaceful methods the English could pot hope to compete successfully with German science and technique, with German commercial and industrial efficiency. Inch by inch the Union Jack has given place in the world of commerce to the flag of the Empire. In peaceable competition, England found herself to be no match for Germany. Nor has the venomous slander of the Germans, which British cables have carried all over the world, accomplished the desired end. The English purse is in jeopardy. Therefore the old method must be resorted to again: "Sink, burn, destroy!"

Just how England would achieve her purpose was still uncertain. Would she continue in her traditional way, and, by entangling others, induce them to fight her battles for her, thus leaving her free to fish in muddy waters? Or would she take a hand in the war herself, for fear the strength of her credulous and infatuated dupes might not prove sufficient, unaided, to accomplish the English purpose? No righteous cause exists for England to take up arms against us. But that has little to do with the matter, as the history of the island nation attests. Lack of a sufficient reason has never deterred England, when a desired end was to be obtained. At such times, the right and the law have ever been matters of supreme indifference to England, nor has she ever failed to find a mantle of hypocritical righteousness with which to clothe her purpose.

Surely, Lord Derby, one of England's ablest statesmen of the nineteenth century, understood his own people well when he said of them in Parliament: Our conduct with regard to other nations is shameful. We insist upon a strict adherence to international law whenever it is to our advantage to do so; when otherwise, we disregard it utterly. The history of marine law, or, I might say, marine lawlessness, is an indelible witness to the unbridled selfishness and greed of the English people and of their government.

Thus Lord Derby.

There is not a nation on earth that has not suffered the consequences of English selfishness and greed,—Spain, whose flourishing commerce and colonial empire were annihilated by the English sword, and who still must endure her thorn in the flesh, Gibraltar; Holland, whose prosperity was drained by the English vampire, and who has England to thank for the position of insignificance which has replaced her former greatness; Denmark, whose fleet was attacked and carried off by the English in 1807, at a time when the two countries were absolutely at peace, and Copenhagen bombarded and destroyed by fire before ever there was a thought of war; China, which in 1840 was overrun with war because the Chinese refused to buy opium of the English merchants; Egypt, which England wrested from the Turkish Empire, and whose people now are compelled to get their dearly bought bread from England, to increase that country's tariff receipts, while, at her orders, the land, in this granary of the ancient world, is planted with cotton instead of grain, to the end that England may be independent of America with regard to this product.

India, where pestilence and famine-typhus, and an enforced payment of an annual tribute of one and one half billions are the blessings bestowed by English culture, and against which the crushed and exploited people of India strive in vain; the Boer States, that were coveted and therefore subjugated by England because of their gold and diamond mines; Turkey, upon the dismemberment of which England has long been bent; France, humiliated at Fashoda; Russia, against whom Japan was incited; Portugal, now no more than England's vassal; Italy, to whom territorial expansion in Africa was denied; even America, where England made the attempt to forbid the construction and fortification of the Panama Canal, and where the public is not allowed to learn of world events except through English sources and according to English interpretation.

Having lost her political hold on America, England fell back upon the principle: "Ignorance is the chief factor in intellectual conflicts as it is in physical strife between nations," and forthwith proceeded to take advantage of her cables in order to surround the "free nation" by such an atmosphere of falsehood that today it is impossible for Americans to form an unbiased opinion, and they can but echo the sentiments of England. With respect to the formation of opinion and judgment, the Americans are in subjection to England intellectually, quite as much as are politically the races that England has subjugated with the sword.

As for English truthfulness, Thomas Carlyle portrays it aptly when he says: Englishmen no longer dare to believe the truth. For two centuries they have been surrounded by falsehood of every kind. They regard the truth as dangerous, and everywhere we see them striving to modify it by bidding a lie go with it, the two harnessed together. This they term the safe middle path.

And so there is hardly a race on the face of the earth that is not wearing shackles, political or moral, that England's unbounded selfishness and greed have forged. With the German Empire only have England's methods failed. Therefore, France and Russia, together with the regicides of Sarajevo as fitting henchmen and accomplices, were now to be employed to achieve England's purpose for her. Should they prove insufficient, however, then England herself would take a hand. Some plausible excuse for making war upon Germany will be trumped up by England to satisfy her own people and the world in general. Hypocritically righteous reasons for her actions England has never been at a loss to find. Today the English purpose will hardly be expressed as candidly as it was two hundred years ago when the destruction of Dutch commerce was the object desired. At that time, when the men who wished to make war upon Holland were seeking for a "reason" for doing so, the English admiral exclaimed: "Reasons? Why should we look for reasons? What we want is more of the commerce that the Dutch now control That is reason enough."

Now it is Germany's turn. As early as 1907, an English publication, *The Saturday Review*, said: England's prosperity will never be assured until Germany has been destroyed. Were Germany to be wiped from the face of the earth tomorrow, there is not an Englishman in the world who would not be the richer for it on the day after tomorrow. Nations have fought for years over territory, or over the right of succession,—why then should they not go to war to secure commerce that is worth so many billions a year to them?

Yes, the English will surely join our enemies, but not until such a time as seems most favourable to them. Whether now, or later, whether by an immediate participation in the war, or not until towards the end, when Germany has been weakened, we cannot tell. But attack us, they surely will. For this is England's war, to which she has been inciting the nations for years past. The last free country is now to feel the onslaught of England's uncurbed selfishness and greed.

"Guns ready!" "Torpedo service ready!" "Engines and auxiliary engines ready!" "Leak service ready!" "Steering service ready!" "Signal and wireless service ready!"

Rapidly, one after the other, the reports from all over the ship were now coming in, and demanded my attention to the exclusion of all further thought and reflection. A quick tour of inspection through the ship assured me that all was in readiness, and I could report to our commander, "The ship is clear for action."

At a speed of fifteen nautical miles we were proceeding toward the Strait of Tchusima. When darkness came on, the war watch was begun on the *Emden*, which is done in the following manner: Half of the men of the crew remain awake and on duty at their posts,—at the guns, at the searchlights and lookouts, in the torpedo room, in the engine and fire rooms, etc., while the others are allowed to go to sleep with their clothes on, and ready, at a moment's notice, to get to their posts. The commander of the ship takes charge of one of these watches, and the other one is in command of the first officer.

After passing through the Strait of Tchusima, the *Emden* steered northward. There was no moon, and the night was pitch black. It was too dark to see anything even in our immediate vicinity. We were, of course, travelling with all lights screened. Not a ray of light was allowed to escape from the ship, nor the least bit of smoke from her funnels. There was a moderate sea running, and the water was unusually bright with phosphorescence. The water churned up by our screws stretched away behind the ship in a shimmering wake of light green. The waves dashing high up against the bow, and the water tumbling and breaking against the sides, splashed the whole ship with a phosphorescent glitter, and made her appear as though she had been dipped into molten gold of a greenish hue. Occasionally, there appeared in the water large shining spots of great length, so that a number of times the lookouts reported undersea boats in sight.

At four o'clock in the morning the port war watch, which I commanded, was relieved. The commander now took charge. The day was just dawning. I had just gone to my cabin, and had lain down to rest, when I was wakened by the shrill call of the alarm bells and the loud

Commander Von Müller

noise of many hurrying feet. "Clear ship for action," the order went echoing from room to room. In an instant everyone was at his post. Were we really to be so fortunate as to fall in, on our very first day, with one of the Russian or French ships that had been reported to us as being in the vicinity of Vladivostok?

By the trembling of the ship we could tell that the engine had been put on high speed. In the gray of the early morning we sighted, ahead of us and a little to the right, a vessel somewhat larger than our own, which was also travelling with screened lights, and looked like a man of war. Our commander ordered a course toward her at high speed. Hardly had she seen us when she turned hard about, took the contrary course, and ran away from us, the dense column of smoke rising from her funnels indicating that her engines were working at maximum power. The pursued ship took a course directly toward the Japanese Islands, lying about ten miles distant. A black cloud of smoke streamed behind her, rested on the water, and, for a while, hid her from sight entirely. We could see nothing of her but the mast tops, and so found it impossible to discover the nature of the vessel with which we were dealing. That she was not a neutral was evident enough from her behaviour. Therefore, after her with full speed!

Meanwhile, daylight had come. The signal: "Stop at once!" was flying at our foremast. When this demand was not complied with after a reasonable time, we fired a blind shell, and when this also failed to have the desired effect, we sent a quick reminder in the form of a couple of sharp shots after her. The fleeing ship could no longer hope to reach the neutral waters of Japan. When our shots fell into the water close beside her, she stopped, turned, and set the Russian colours in all her topmasts. So, on the very first night after the war had begun, we had taken our first prize. It was the Russian volunteer steamer *Rjesan*. In time of peace she had plied as a passenger steamer between Shanghai and Vladivostok. She was now to be armed with guns and to serve as an auxiliary cruiser. She was a speedy and very new ship, built in the German shipyards of Schichau.

In the sea that was running, the *Emden* and her prize rolled badly. It was therefore no easy matter to get the cutter, that was to carry the prize crew from the *Emden* to the *Rjesan*, into the water. There was danger that it would be pounded to pieces against the sides of the ships. However, everything passed off satisfactorily. In a short time we saw the officer of the prize crew, followed by a number of men, all armed with pistols, climbing up the gangway ladder. The Russian flag was hauled down, and in its place the German colours were run up.

As the steamer was one that could serve our own purposes excellently well—she could be transformed into a very good German auxiliary cruiser—our commander decided not to destroy her, but instead to take her to Tsingtao. At a speed of fifteen miles we made our way southward. Behind us, in our wake, followed the *Rjesan*. A commanding officer with a prize crew of twelve men remained aboard of her, to make certain that the service of the ship and the engines, etc., would be according to our wishes.

Twice the Russian captain of the *Rjesan* made a vehement protest against the capture of his ship, saying that she was a peaceable merchantman, that to seize her was an unprecedented violation of law, and that he could not understand it at all. However, when we asked him why, if that was the case, he had tried to run away from us, he had nothing more to say. His knowledge of maritime law was evidently nothing to boast of. Our commander sent him word that his case would be decided at Tsingtao, whither we were going.

The *Emden* did not, however, steer the most direct course to Tsingtao. Hardly had the Russian captain of our prize observed this, when he protested afresh, demanding to be taken to port by the shortest route. The reason for this was, of course, his apprehension that, on the course we were following, we would be likely to meet other Russian ships that were in the vicinity. And, it must be admitted, this *was* our intention. To be sure, we had no information with regard to the course that the Russian ships were taking, but, judging from the violent remonstrances of the captain, we concluded that there was good prospect that we should come up with one or two of them before long. Much to our regret, however, not one came in sight. Naturally, no regard was given to the captain's protests, and our commander sent him word informing him that the *Emden's'* course was no concern of his, and reminding him of what are the usual consequences of insubordination on board ship. After that, we heard nothing more from our Russian friend. He probably consoled himself after his own fashion.

From the newspapers, we had learned that the main body of the French fleet, consisting of the armoured cruisers *Montcalm* and *Dupleix*, besides a number of torpedo boat destroyers, was lying somewhere off Vladivostok. With these ships the *Emden* must not be allowed to come in contact by daylight. As we were rounding the southern extremity of Corea, the lookout in the top suddenly sang out, "Seven smoke clouds in sight astern!"

To make quite sure of it, the commander sent me aloft. I, too, could distinctly see seven separate columns of smoke, together with the upper structure of a small vessel, the one nearest to us, just above the horizon. Upon hearing my report, the commander gave orders to change our course. We swept a wide circle, and so avoided the enemy. Without meeting with hindrance of any kind, we arrived at Tsingtao.

On the way we caught up an interesting wireless message. The Reuter Agency, so celebrated for its rigid adherence to facts, was sending a telegram abroad, informing the credulous world that the *Emden* had been sunk. How many sympathetic people must have shuddered as they read,—and so did we, of course!

During the following night, our prize occasioned us some further trouble. Naturally, her lights, as well as our own, had to be screened. It was a much easier matter to give orders to that effect, however, than to see to it that they were carried out. On the steamer were several women passengers, who, from the outset, were filled with mortal terror as to what the barbarous Germans would do with them. Most of them were fat Russian Jewesses. Every few minutes they would turn on the electric lights in their cabins, so that finally there was nothing left for the officer of the prize crew to do but to have the electric light cable in the engine capped. Then they managed to find lights elsewhere, but this also could not, of course, be tolerated.

Upon our arrival at Tsingtao, the *Rjesan* was overhauled. The ship was an entirely new one, and so had not been in the hands of the Russians long enough to give them opportunity to spoil the engine which was of first-class German workmanship. Our prize could still run at a speed of seventeen nautical miles. So she was equipped with guns, was manned by a German crew, and continued her career as the German auxiliary cruiser *Cormoran*.

At Tsingtao preparations for war were in full swing. The harbour had been mined, the forts all along the water front had been manned, and vigorous work was under way in the harbour itself. In the moles lay a large number of German steamers. Some of them were being fitted up as auxiliary cruisers, while others were being loaded with coal in order to serve our squadron as coal tenders. Our commander found orders awaiting him from the admiral of our squadron. Count von Spee, who, with the armoured cruisers, *Scharnhorst* and *Gneisenau*,' and the small cruiser, *Nürnberg*,' was in the South Pacific, steering northward. The *Emden's* orders were to join this squadron at a stated point of meeting in the South Pacific.

Chapter 2

Southward Bound

Aboard our ship there was much to be done, and it kept us busy throughout that day and the following night. Coal had to be taken on to the limit of our capacity, and as many supplies as possible of all kinds stored away on board. The ship's personnel had to be supplemented, and other final preparations for war made. At sunrise on the following day the *Emden* left Tsingtao in the company of a large number of German ships, all bound for the south, where they were to join the admiral's squadron.

In the harbour unbounded enthusiasm reigned. Everyone ashore was envious of us. If the war was to be with France and Russia only, Tsingtao could hardly be expected to take any part in it. For the fortress itself, no concern whatever was felt, as, from the ocean side, it was protected by good and sufficient defences that would make a seizure by war ships impossible. To be sure, the land defences, in so far as they were such at all, consisted of very small and modest earthworks, sufficient only to serve as protection against an assault by infantry. But an attack from the land side was not to be expected, as Tsingtao was entirely surrounded by neutral Chinese territory.

With fair weather and a smooth sea the *Emden* slipped out of the harbour moles. Our band played "The Watch on the Rhine." The entire crew was on deck, singing as the band played. Cheers rang from ship to shore, and back again. Everyone was confident and in high spirits. In a small way it was a repetition of the scenes which, on a grand scale, manifested the nation's devotion to country in Germany when it was learned that war was inevitable.

Cautiously the *Emden* made her way between the mines which barred the entrance to the harbour. The sun had just risen. Behind us lay Tsingtao, the gem of the far East, brightened by the golden-red beams of the young day—a picture of peace. Along the shore could be seen the long line of neat and tastily built houses, the whole scene dominated by the height on which stood the signal tower. In the background rose the brown hills, their sombre colour relieved by the fresh green of the young trees with which they had been planted.

From out the delicately pink mist of the early morning rose the church steeple bearing the cross aloft. Farther to the right were to be seen the trim, well-kept barracks, the government buildings, and the bathing beach,—the whole picture rimmed by the white line of the surf that broke upon the rocky shore with the incessant rising and falling of the sea. Glittering diamonds and pearls were strewn with a lavish hand by old Neptune on the hem of earth's fair garment. Nature's charm and German industry had combined to produce a picture of bewitching beauty in the midst of this otherwise forbidding and rugged region. As we gazed, there was not one of us who was not conscious of a strange tugging at his heart. But duty called with an imperative voice. Therefore, farewell to the fair scene we were leaving behind us! For us, it was, "Onward, to the South!"

We were accompanied by the *Markomannia*, the other ships taking different courses. The *Markomannia* remained our faithful companion for a number of months.

On our way to the South Pacific we learned, by wireless, of the rupture in the relations between Germany and England, and of the latter's declaration of war. It was not unexpected by us, and if we were surprised at all, it was that this wirepuller among the nations, who had so often plunged the others into misery, was now actually going to risk her own bones in serious conflict, for the first time in a hundred years. A few days later we learned of Japan's remarkable ultimatum, without its causing us any special anxiety. It might as well all be done up at one and the same time, was the general feeling among us.

When the *Emden* left Tsingtao, England and Japan had as yet not declared war against Germany. Nevertheless, soon afterward, we read in some English newspapers that our "escape" from Tsingtao had been made possible only by the fact that we flew the English flag while passing a blockading Japanese cruiser, and that we greeted this quasi brother-in-arms with three cheers.

We wondered whether this report might have had its origin in the circumstance that English and Japanese cruisers had already been ordered to Tsingtao, before ever a declaration of war had been made.

In any case, the story is absurd. For, aside from the fact that under no condition would we have dishonoured our brave ship by flying the English flag, we would never have passed the Japanese cruiser without sending her a torpedo as a greeting.

'Tis strange how the practice of systematic and continued misrepresentation warps the judgement.

On the twelfth of August, in the evening, we had reached the vicinity of the island where we were to join our cruiser squadron, and soon we fell in with some of the ships that were serving as outposts. As we approached the group of assembled war ships, we saw the stanch cruisers *Scharnhorst* and *Gneisenau* lying in the midst of them, each with a coal tender alongside, and engaged in coaling. To the left lay the slender *Nürnberg*, also busy with taking on coal. Distributed about the bay, many larger and smaller auxiliary ships and tenders of the squadron could be seen. The *Emden* was ordered to an anchorage close beside the flagship, in the right-hand half of the bay. Rousing cheers were sent from deck to deck, as we passed by the other ships, and soon our anchor rattled seaward, and to the bottom,—it was to be the last time for many a long day.

Our commander went aboard the flagship to report to the admiral of the squadron, and to submit to him the proposal that the *Emden* be detached from the squadron, and be sent to the Indian Ocean, to raid the enemy's commerce.

On the following day the squadron steered an easterly course, the ships keeping a long line, one behind the other, with all the coal tenders bringing up the rear. The Admiral had, for the present, reserved his decision with regard to our commander's proposition, and we were all impatient to learn what it would be. At last, toward noon, signal flags were seen running up on the flagship. They read "*Emden* detached. Wish you good luck!" Sweeping a wide curve, the *Emden* withdrew from the long line of war ships, a signal conveying her commander's thanks for the good wishes of the admiral fluttering at her mast head. There was still another signal from the commanding officer of the squadron, ordering the *Markomannia* to attend the *Emden*. Ere long we had lost sight of the other ships of the squadron, which now were steering a course contrary to our own, and we all knew full well that we should never meet again.

It was a long journey to our new field of action. That we had no information with regard to our relations with Japan was a source of annoyance, as we did not know whether we were or were not at war with that country. The German wireless apparatus at Station Jap had already been destroyed by the English. After a week's run we met at sea the German steamer *Princess Alice.* We took off a few reservists, and then sent her on to Manila. A little later, far out at sea, we met the little German gunboat *Geier.* As our signal connections had been destroyed, she had no news of the war to give us, in so far as England and Japan were concerned. We remained together for but a short time, only just long enough to exchange what news we each had. Then the *Geier* passed on eastward, on her way to join the squadron, while we continued in the direction of our future hunting ground.

These days were strenuous ones for our men, as the war watch was continued without intermission, in order that the ship might be ready at a moment's notice for any emergency. There was no opportunity to give the crew even a short season of rest. For us, there was not one harbour of refuge where we might lie free from danger.

Very regretfully we allowed a Japanese steamer, that we met on the way, to proceed undisturbed, as we did not know, at the time, whether or not we were at war with Japan. In passing, the Jap greeted us most obsequiously, dipping her flag especially low, in the supposition, no doubt, that we were an Englishman. We left her salute unanswered.

To reach the open sea, our course now led us through a number of narrow water ways. These straits swarmed with fishing boats and other small sea craft. The nights were bright with moonlight, which made it possible to recognize the *Emden* at a considerable distance. To meet so many boats was a source of anxiety to our commander, who expressed himself as apprehensive that our presence in these waters, and our probable course also, would be noised about by some of these vessels. All English ships have either two or four funnels, whereas the *Emden* had three.

The happy thought came to me that much might be gained if the *Emden* were provided with a fourth funnel. So I quickly ordered a number of deck-runners to be fetched out. Deck-runners are strips of heavy sail-cloth about two metres in width, and, under ordinary circumstances, are used to protect the linoleum deck. Up above, a wooden post was fastened at the proper place in front of our forward funnel, and then our counterfeit funnel was placed in position around it. Viewed from the side, it made an excellent impression. From the front, it must be admitted, its appearance left much to be desired. It lacked the well-rounded proportions of its fellows, for it was only a few millimetres in diameter. However, in the hurry to have it ready for use in the coming night, nothing better could be put together.

I suggested to our commander that, given more time, I could produce a much better looking fourth funnel, and he approved of the undertaking. So, on the following morning, we set to work. Out of wooden laths and sail-cloth we soon had constructed a funnel of most elegant appearance, and, when it had been placed in position, the *Emden* was the exact counterpart of the British cruiser *Yarmouth*. It was with this precise object in view that we had given the funnel an oval shape, as I was aware that the *Yarmouth* carried such an one. Our tender, the *Markomannia*, was then sent out to the one side of us, and, with signals, she gave us directions as to how we could improve the position of our fourth funnel. We then placed marks on the light steel ropes which served to hoist the funnel into position, so that, at any time of the day or night, and at a moment's notice, our counterfeit funnel could be neatly and properly placed.

In this way, by the end of the first week in September, we had got as far as the Bay of Bengal. For a period of about five days an English man-of-war, most likely the *Minotaur*, kept a course close beside our own, which we learned from the frequent wireless messages that we caught up. Gradually, her messages became less distinct, and then ceased altogether. At no time had she come within sight of us.

Chapter 3

On the Chase

It was not until the night of September tenth that our work began in real earnest. A steamer came in sight, and we approached her very cautiously, so as to give her a closer inspection. Quietly, and with lights screened, we crept up behind our intended victim. Our commander ordered an approach to within one hundred metres of the steamer, which was peacefully and unsuspectingly proceeding on her course, and, after the manner of merchantmen, was paying little heed to anything except what was ahead of her and showing lights. Suddenly, through the stillness of the perfectly calm night, rang out our challenge through the speaking trumpet:

"Stop at once! Do not use your wireless! We are sending a boat!"

The steamer did not seem to realize what was meant by this order. Perhaps she did not expect, here in the heart of Indian waters, to run across an enemy's man-of-war. Or she may have thought it the voice of a sea god, and therefore no concern of hers. At any rate, she continued on her way undeterred. So, to explain the situation, we sent a blank shot whizzing past her. This made an impression, and, pell-mell, her engines were reversed—we truly regretted the start we had given her dozing engineers—and with her siren she howled out her willingness to obey our order.

One of our cutters, with a prize crew in it, glided swiftly to water, and thence to the steamer, of which we thus took possession. An unpleasant surprise was now in store for us, for soon there came flashing back to us a signal given by one of the men of our prize crew: "This is the Greek steamer, *Pontoporros*."

Our first steamer, and a neutral! Now it would be but a few days before the entire coast would know that a German war ship was abroad in the Indian Ocean. The very best of prizes might escape us on account of it. But, as good fortune would have it, our classic captive was loaded with contraband. She was carrying coal to British ports. She was therefore most welcome, to supplement the *Markomannia*, whose coal bunkers were already half empty, and we gladly added her to our squadron, which now consisted of three ships. They were not long to remain the only ones, however.

The *Pontoporros* was loaded with coal from India, the very dirtiest coal in the world. I had hoped, as our store of supplies diminished, to be able to replenish it from the cargoes of our prizes as we captured them. It was now six weeks since the *Emden* had put in at a port, and in all that time we had, of course, not had an opportunity to take on supplies of any kind. On board ship the first officer is, in a way, the housekeeper, for it is his duty to attend to all the details of fitting out the ship with supplies of every description. Before running out from Tsingtao, I had, in so far as possible, packed the ship with everything that I had thought necessary or useful. But now, during the last few days, it had developed that our supply of soap was getting alarmingly low. The usually very generous quantity of soap allowed each man had therefore shrunk to proportions that approached the vanishing point, and it looked as though in a couple of weeks washing would be classed among the luxuries of life aboard the *Emden*.

I had therefore, in jest, entreated our commander to capture, as our first prize, a ship loaded with soap, instead of which we now got this cargo of dirty Indian coal. My disappointment was so great that I could not refrain from reproachfully calling our commander's attention to it, and, with a laugh, he promised to do his best toward providing us with the much needed soap. And he kept his word.

On the morning of the eleventh of September, only a few hours after we had made the first addition to our squadron, there appeared, forward, a large steamer, which, in the supposition that we were an English man-of-war, manifested her delight at meeting us by promptly running up a large English flag while still a long way off.

We could not help wondering what sort of expression her captain's face wore when we ran up the German colours, and politely requested him to remain with us for a while.

The steamer hailed from Calcutta, had been requisitioned to serve as an English transport for carrying troops from Colombo to France, and was fitted out with an abundance of excellent supplies. A very pleasing surprise awaited us, and one for which we were indebted to the English native love of cleanliness, a virtue which no one will be inclined to dispute. In this case it had manifested itself in storing away so much soap in the ship, that for us, with our small crew, it was sufficient to supply our needs for at least a year, even though we should be spendthrift in the use of this indispensable requisite of modern civilization.

We also found aboard the ship a very handsome race horse. By a shot through the head, this noble creature was spared the agony of death by drowning. But our sympathy was hardly sufficient to extend to all the many mounts for artillery, which occupied as many neatly numbered stalls that had been built into the ship. They had to be left to become the prey of sharks a half hour later. The ship's crew was sent aboard our "junkman." The ship that did junkman's duty for us was either a recently captured vessel that was travelling with nothing but ballast in her hold, and consequently was of little value, or else one that was carrying neutral cargo, the sinking of which would have entailed unnecessary expense, as, when the war is over, an indemnity has to be paid for all neutral cargo destroyed. Our "junkman" always followed the *Emden*, until there were as many people gathered aboard her as she could carry. When full, she was discharged, to steam away to the nearest port. At this time the *Pontoporros* was doing "junkman's" service.

During the next few days our business flourished. It was carried on in this way: As soon as a steamer came in sight, she was stopped, and one of our officers, accompanied by ten men, was sent aboard her. It was their duty to get the steamer ready to be sunk, and to arrange for the safe transfer of the passengers and crew. As a rule, while we were still occupied with this, the mast head of the next ship would appear above the horizon. There was no need of giving chase. When the next steamer had come near enough to us, the *Emden* steamed off to meet her, and sent her a friendly signal by which she was induced to join our other previously captured ships. Again an officer and men were sent off, boarded her, got her ready to be sunk, and attended to the transfer of all hands aboard her, etc., and, by the time this was accomplished, the mast head of the third ship had usually come in sight. Again the *Emden* went to meet her, and so the game went on.

There were times when in this way we had gathered about us from five to six steamers. Of these, the first arrival would be showing only the funnel above water; the next was probably up to the deck under water; the condition of the third one still appeared to be normal, although a slight swaying from side to side showed that she, too, was getting full. The passengers of these captured ships made surprising acquaintances on board our junkmen.

In this way we cleaned up the whole region from Ceylon to Calcutta. In addition to our old companion, the *Markomannia*, we were now accompanied by the Greek collier *Pontoporros*, which, in the meanwhile, had relinquished the role of "junkman" to the *Cabigna*. The latter was an English steamer carrying an American cargo, the destruction of which would have resulted in nothing but unnecessary charges.

The *Cabigna* continued with us for several days, although she, the *Markomannia*, and the *Pontoporros* were not the only companions of the *Emden* during that night. We had captured more prizes, whose destruction, however, was deferred to the following day in consideration of the passengers, because of the darkness, and the high seas running. All told, we had six attendants that night.

Three of these disappeared in the sea on the coming morning, and the *Cabigna* was discharged to land her passengers.

Aboard the *Cabigna* were the wife and little child of the captain. The position at sea, where the other steamers had been sent to the bottom, was so far distant from the nearest shore that it would have been quite impossible for any boats to have reached land. Before the captain of the *Cabigna* had been told that he would be allowed to proceed, and in the assumption that his ship also was to be sunk, he begged that he might be allowed to take a revolver with him for the protection of his wife and child. This is a typical case to illustrate the absurd ideas entertained by the British public as a result of the persistent slander of the Germans in which the English newspapers have indulged. According to the representations of the English press it would have been all of a piece with German custom if we had set these women and children out in open boats, hundreds of miles out at sea, to leave them there to starve.

When the captain was informed that it was not our purpose to destroy his ship, he was overcome with joy. I, myself, was aboard his ship for several hours, and he could not find words sufficient to express his gratitude, begging me to convey his thanks to our commander, and finally handing me a letter to deliver to him. In it he thanked us once more for the "humane" treatment which he and his family had received, at our hands, saying that the officers and men of the prize crew placed in command of his ship had all conducted themselves like gentlemen, that he could not find sufficient words of praise for the deportment of the Germans, that he would never forget the consideration shown him by our commander, who, he said, had treated him with as much kindliness and courtesy as it is possible for one seaman to extend to another in an emergency, even in time of peace, and he further assured us that he would do all in his power to have the truth made public through the English newspapers,

I had a long conversation with the captain's wife, also, and she expressed sentiments much like those contained in her husband's letter to our commander. When she discovered, from something I said, that my oil-skins were going to pieces, she pressed me to accept her husband's. Besides this, upon learning that our supply of smoking tobacco was getting low, she urged us to take as many cigarettes and as much smoking tobacco with us as we could carry. These, she declared, were but trifling gifts in comparison with the gratitude she felt.

It is hardly necessary to say that we took with us neither the tobacco nor the oil-skins.

At the time that the *Cabigna* was discharged, her deck was full of passengers, all people from the steamers we had captured. At our order, "You may proceed!" three cheers—"Hurrah! Hurrah! Hurrah!"—rang back to us, one for the commander, one for the officers, and one for the crew of H. M. S. *Emden*, in which every person on the crowded deck joined. How many souls the *Cabigna* carried can best be estimated from the description of her entrance into Calcutta, as given in an English newspaper, which, sometime later, fell into our hands. It stated that no one would have supposed the *Cabigna* to be a merchantman, but rather would have taken her to be a training ship, so crowded was her deck. There were, at the time, about four hundred persons aboard the ship.

In the further progress of our activities we never failed to get three cheers from our discharged "junkmen," as they departed with their collection of passengers from captured steamers. Hence it would appear that it is customary with Englishmen to cheer barbarians who murder little children and wantonly slay men and women.

This seems a fitting place to speak about the attitude taken by the Englishmen when we captured their ships. Most of them behaved very sensibly. After they had recovered from the first shock of surprise, they usually passed into the stage of unrestrained indignation at their government, at which they swore roundly. With but one exception, they never offered any resistance to the sinking of their ships. We always allowed them time enough to collect and take with them their personal possessions. They usually devoted most of this time to making certain that their precious supply of whiskey was not wasted on the fishes. I can say with truth that seldom did we send off a wholly sober lot of passengers on any one of our "junkmen." In general, they had an eye open to "business," and made every reasonable effort to make certain that the advantages of German commerce raiding should be extended to the ships of their competitors among the steamship lines. For instance, upon leaving his ship, the captain of an English steamer would say something like this: "Tell me, have you run across the steamer 'X'?" to which we would reply, "No."

"What," the captain would then exclaim, "you haven't seen her! Why, she steers a course only seven miles to the south, and is only two hours behind me!"

In this way we usually knew the name of the next ship to appear, long before her mast head had come in sight above the horizon, and, moreover, it gave us opportunity to avoid annoying meetings with neutrals.

One captain was especially amusing. His was the unenviable duty of taking a bucket-dredger from England to Australia. No seafaring man can help sympathizing with the unfortunate who has to conduct one of these rolling tubs, with a speed of not more than four nautical miles at best, all the way from Europe down to Australia. And so, from a purely humane standpoint, we could fully appreciate this English captain's joy at being captured. Rarely have I seen anyone jump so high for joy. He must have been a past master in the art of jumping to be able to keep his feet in spite of the terrible rolling of his ship. Tears of gratitude coursed down his weathered cheeks as he exclaimed, "Thank God, that the old tub is gone! The five hundred pounds I was to have for taking her to Australia were paid me in advance."

A seafaring man is always strangely moved by the sight of a sinking ship. We, who heretofore had always done everything within our power to help any ship in distress, were no exception, and never failed to experience a peculiar sensation when our duty compelled us to destroy the ships, and we saw them sink. It was usually accomplished in this way:

One of our men was sent down into the engine room of the captured vessel to unscrew the cap to one of the large pipes that open outward. Hereupon the sea would instantly rush into the engine room in so powerful a stream that it forced its way in, in a column of water twice a man's height, and with a circumference of a man's girth. The water-tight door leading into the boiler room was always opened and fastened back, so that it had to remain so. In this way we made certain that two large compartments of the ship would fill with water. In addition to these two, we opened two more to the sea, by means of blasts, which were always set off at night, or else by two well placed shots. For a while the ship would then lunge from side to side, as though uncertain as to what was expected of her under these unusual circumstances. Then she settled deeper and deeper into the water, until the sea washed the railing.

The waves swept greedily over the deck of the vessel doomed to destruction. Unseen hands seemed to be pulling and hauling to draw their victim more quickly down into the deep, A shiver ran through the whole structure, as though the ship were shaking with fear, or as if she were making one last, desperate effort to escape from her impending fate. Then there was evident submission to the inevitable, and the final collapse. The bow dipped into the water, the masts came flat upon it, and the screws and rudder rose high in air. From the funnels came a last puff of smoke and escaping steam. For a moment the ship stood on end, upright in the water, and then shot like an arrow into the deep.

The last resisting hatches and bulkheads of the stern were burst asunder by the force of the compressed air, which, where it escaped through the ventilators and side windows, forced the water out with it in jets like fountains, that rose several metres high, and were scattered in spray by the pressure of the escaping air. A swirl of rushing waters where the ship had disappeared; then the sea closed over her, and she was seen no more. A moment later, as a last token from the vanished ship, a few loose spars and beams, a boat or two, and other like wreckage rose to the surface. Long heavy timbers shot upright out of the water, like arrows from a bow, jumping to a height of several metres above the surface of the sea. When all was over, a large oil spot marked the place where the ship had disappeared, and a crushed boat, a few life-preservers, timbers, and the like floated about. Then the *Emden* steered toward the next mast head to come in sight.

The Englishmen were always very grateful because we allowed them every opportunity to secure and take with them all their personal possessions. For this they gave us full credit in their newspapers. It is probably not too much to say that toward the close of the year 1914 the *Emden* was the most popular ship in East Indian waters. Generally speaking, the English showed little understanding of the war. It is not with them, as it is with us, a people's war, and to a great extent they look upon it with indifference. This makes it possible for them to view the achievements of their friends, and their foes as well, from the sporting side of the situation, and so accounts, in part at least, for the rather remarkable circumstance that our commander and his ship received praise and acclamation from all the newspapers of India. The *Gentleman Captain* was the name by which he was known, and in the newspapers it was said that he "played the game" and was "playing it well."

We always tried to be very considerate of all passengers who were at all civil—and there were but few who were not so—and rendered them every service possible, frequently at the cost of much valuable time. I am reminded of one instance in particular when, just before a steamer was to be destroyed, a young Englishman came to me, begging me to save for him his only possession in the world, and one to which he was wholly devoted,—a motor wheel. It was no easy matter to find the wheel among all the many articles that were packed in the hold of the ship, but we got it out, and, together with its happy owner, it was safely carried in the steam launch, which made an extra trip for the purpose, over to the "junkman," where both wheel and owner were comfortably stowed away.

But there was another Englishman who did not fare as well at our hands. He was a particularly aristocratic gentleman, the "traffic master" at Calcutta, and was on his way to Colombo with a large steamer which he was intending to turn over to the government for use as a transport ship for troops. He was not permitted to carry out his intention, and over this he was very wroth. It has been my experience that when it comes to a matter of business, all Englishmen, even those of almost amiable temper, are very easily irritated. While the ship was being made ready to be sent to the bottom, this gentleman was engaged in packing his numerous and large patent leather trunks, which he piled in a great heap up on deck. Then, with a high and mighty air, as befitting one of the British rulers of the sea, he paced the bridge, his pipe in the corner of his mouth, and his hands in the pockets of his large checked trousers. He cast scornful glances down at us "Germans." To his pile of trunks he paid no further attention, seemingly taking it for granted that, when the proper moment arrived, we would wait upon him to get orders as to what was to be done with them.

Finally all hands had left the ship, taking with them their various belongings, and he was the only person still on board. We were ready to sink the ship, but the traffic master, in "splendid isolation" and big checked trousers, with his pipe in his mouth, was still pacing the ship's bridge. He was informed that it was high time for him to leave the ship. His only reply was a mute gesture,—for which he was obliged to take his hand out of his pocket,—a jerk of his thumb in the direction of his pile of trunks that, in solitary grandeur, was now the sole remaining ornament of the deck. He evidently assumed that his royal gesture would be all-sufficient to remind us of our duty, and that we would instantly stand ready to obey the orders of the "traffic master of Calcutta" with regard to his trunks.

Our men misunderstood him, however, and calmly assured him that he need have no anxiety for his trunks, for, judging from recent experiences, they would sink fast enough without any assistance from them, and that there was reason to believe that the same fate would overtake him, if he did not leave the ship at once. The last boat was about to put off.

Hereupon the traffic master came down, first of all from the height of his English superiority, and then from the height of the ship's bridge. With his own hands he saved at least the smallest one of his collection of trunks, and, perspiring with the exertion, carried it off with him as he left the ship. Our men followed him with their hands in their trousers' pockets, and a cigarette in the corner of their mouths.

The store of provisions with which we started out had, of course, long since come to an end. But, thanks to the kind forethought of the English, the steamers we captured were always so well stocked with canned goods, put up by the best of English firms, that it was fortunate that our men were blessed with good appetites, else it would have been difficult for them, in this respect, to have carried out one of the first rules of warfare, *viz*. that under all circumstances the enemy's stores must be destroyed. In this connection we demonstrated, by sufficient and agreeable experiment, that conserves and other like delicacies are excellent food for sailors, and need not be omitted from their rations on account of the liquor in which they are put up.

In the vicinity of Calcutta we had an undesired meeting with a steamer by the name of *Loredano*. It was not at all necessary for her to run up her flag to establish her nationality, for the dirt, that was everywhere in evidence, proclaimed her from afar to be an Italian. We were obliged to allow this neutral ship to proceed on her way, since a close inspection failed to reveal anything of the nature of contraband. It happened that she arrived on the scene of action just at a time when a collection of ships was about to start on a course for the bottom of the sea. When the last of these ill-fated steamers had disappeared, and the *Emden* was leaving for elsewhere, we could see, on looking back, that the Italians were eagerly engaged in fishing up some floating bales of tea, a part of a large cargo of tea that one of the steamers we had just sunk was carrying. We wondered whether our Italian friends hoped to find their contents to be macaroni. We were not at all disposed to grudge them the fruits of their fishing, but were very far from approving their later conduct, for on the following day this "neutral" steamer undertook to send out wireless messages announcing to all shipping in the surrounding waters that the *Emden* was near. This was a violation of international law, which prohibits neutrals from participating in or interfering with any act of war.

When we had garnered all that the Bay of Bengal here had to offer us, a circumstance which we learned from the fact that day after day not a ship came in sight, we decided to seek another field of action, and betook ourselves to the other side of the Bay, toward Rangoon. Here our first misfortune awaited us,—there were no ships abroad. That all shipping was being held in the harbours on our account was the explanation, but this we did not know until later, when we read it in the newspapers.

Nevertheless there was one happy result to be placed to the credit of our reputation, in that we found it an easy matter to persuade a Norwegian steamer temporarily to assume the *rôle* of "junkman" for us, and we could thus rid ourselves of the last of our undesired guests.

Because of our detour to Rangoon, we had been seen by no one for the whole of one week. In wise forethought for the welfare of their subjects, the discreet British government authorities in India utilized this interim to gladden the hearts of their patiently waiting countrymen by officially announcing to them that the *Emden* had at last been destroyed by one of the sixteen ships that were hunting her, and that shipping could therefore be resumed without fear of further disturbance. Naturally, but unfortunately for us, we could not know of this at the time, but learned it later from the newspapers.

As no merchantmen made their appearance in the waters we were ranging, we returned to our former hunting ground, along the east coast of the Indian peninsula. Our commander decided to put the oil tanks at Madras to the test. On the eighteenth of September, in the evening, the *Emden* entered the harbour. It so happened that this was the day after the one on which the joyful tidings of the *Emden's* destruction had been officially announced. To celebrate the happy occasion, a large company had assembled for dinner at the Club, As we were not aware of this, it was hardly our fault that the *Emden's* shells fell into the soup. Had we known of the dinner party, we would, of course, gladly have deferred our attack until another day, as it is the part of wisdom never to exasperate the enemy unnecessarily, A due regard should always be shown for sacred institutions, and *dinner* is an institution with regard to which the English are always keenly sensitive.

We approached to within 3000 metres of Madras. The harbour light was shining peacefully. It rendered us good service as we steered toward shore, for which we again take this opportunity to express our gratitude to the British Indian government. A searchlight revealed to us the object of our quest,—the oil tanks, painted white and ornamented with a stripe of red. A couple of shells sent in that direction, a quick upleaping of tongues of bluish-yellow flame, streams of liquid fire pouring out through the holes made by our shots, an enormous black cloud of dense smoke,—and, following the advice of the old adage, "A change is good for everybody," we had sent several millions' worth of the enemy's property up into the air, instead of down into the sea, as heretofore.

It seems that shots were fired after us from Madras, although, at the time, we did not know where the shells came from. There were not many, however, and they were poorly aimed. The English newspapers said of us in this connection that, when we were fired at, we quickly put out all our lights, and, turning tail, got away in all haste. To this I would say that, as a matter of course, we made our approach to Madras without lights of any kind; furthermore, that neither our commander nor myself were at the time aware that we were being fired at, and that the shots were observed only by the officers at the stern of the ship. It had not entered our minds, therefore, to run from the firing. In so far as our lights were concerned, our tactics were just the reverse of those that were ascribed to us. As soon as we had fired the necessary number of shots, we lit up the ship, that is, we made a point of showing as much light as possible at her stern, while we took a northerly course. Then, after a sufficient time had elapsed, we shut off all lights and steered southward.

The flames at Madras illumined our course for a long while. On the following day, when we were ninety nautical miles distant from

Madras, we could still see a dense cloud of black smoke rising from the burning oil.

Past Pondicherry, and around the island of Ceylon, we continued our course, steadily steering westward to reach the other side of India, and honour that coast with our presence.

As we learned from the newspapers some time later, our attack upon Madras resulted in a general exodus of the European population from the coast region into the interior of the country. Furthermore, as a result of it, the English instituted a searchlight service all along the coast, that is, all night long searchlights played over the whole area of water lying just beyond the ports. This solved a good many navigation problems for us, and again we would express our belated thanks to the efficient British government authorities of India.

On the twenty-sixth day of September the *Emden* lay just outside of the port of Colombo. As we were cruising back and forth, suddenly, in the path of the searchlight, appeared a dark shadow that roused our lively interest. It looked rather dangerous at first, but, upon closer inspection, appeared more to our liking. It was an English steamer, crammed up to her very throat with sugar. Her captain was so exasperated at the idea of being captured right in the path of the searchlights of his own home port, which had been fortified for defence, and actually within range of the guns of the British forts, that he attempted to defy our orders. For him the unhappy consequence of this ill-advised burst of patriotism was that he was not allowed time enough to look for so much as a handkerchief to take with him.

Within five minutes the entire crew of the steamer was taken off her, and housed aboard our "junkman." The captain and his engineer received the distinction of being temporarily assigned to a cell aboard H. M. S. *Emden*. Ten minutes later the sugar cargo was adding sweetness to the supper of all the fish in the surrounding water. Later, we read in the newspapers the most incredible pirate tales which this captain had told of the *Emden*. Although admitting that he had been well treated, he nevertheless complained that the respect due his standing had not been shown him. We wondered whether he had expected the *Emden's* commander to relinquish his cabin to him. Moreover; he spoke very disparagingly of the *Emden's* condition in so far as cleanliness was concerned. He said she was not only dirty, but scratched and dented as well.

To this accusation we are obliged to plead guilty. To be unintermittently at sea for weeks, to take on coal from other steamers at sea, and carry it in such quantities that it has to be stored on deck, is apt to leave its marks on a ship. Had I known beforehand that we were going to have so distinguished a guest aboard, my pride, as first officer of the ship, undoubtedly would have induced me to make strenuous efforts to have the ship cleaned and freshly painted for his special benefit.

In addition, this critical gentleman said of us that the men of our crew looked starved and wore an air of dejection. To this I can but say that it would be doing a gross injustice to the provisioning of the English ships we had captured to say that our men looked hungry. And their air of dejection must have impressed our guest so forcibly while they were executing their best hornpipes for his benefit to such tunes as "That was in Schöneberg in the lovely month of May," or "*Snuten und Poten*," played by the ship's band at the regular after-dinner concerts.

Later, after our unwilling guest had left us, and was on his way, aboard our next "junkman" that was sent off with a full load, he may not have fared as well as he did on the *Emden*. The officer of the prize crew that remained on board the "junkman," up to the moment when she was discharged, told us that the officers of the defunct sugar steamer were furious with their captain, saying that, whereas he was fully insured, they were not, and therefore his foolish show of resistance had cost them all they owned. When the captain came on board the "junkman," his officers were standing at the gangway ladder, with sleeves rolled up, waiting to receive him. He may have had reason to wish himself back on the *Emden*.

Meanwhile the coaling question had come to be a source of annoyance to us. Our faithful *Markomannia* had no more coal to give us. To be sure, our prize, the *Pontoporros*, with her cargo of coal from India, was still with us. But this Indian coal is far from being desirable fuel, as it not only clogs the fire kettles with dirt, but, while it gives out a minimum of heat, it sends forth a maximum of smoke, and so our prize was not an unmixed joy to us. However, this vexed coal question was happily solved for us by the English Admiralty in a most satisfactory manner. Before many days had passed, a fine large steamer of 7000 tonnage, loaded with the best of Welsh coal, *en route* for Hong Kong, and destined for their own use, was relinquished to us by the English in a most unselfish manner.

So, for the present, we were most generously supplied with the best of fuel, and all further anxiety on this account was dismissed to the uncertain future. The captain of our new coal-laden prize seemed to have no scruples with regard to transferring himself, together with his ship, into German service. Willingly and faithfully he co-operated with the officer of the prize crew that was, of course, placed in command of his ship, all the while cheerfully whistling "Rule, Britannia."

In the meantime, even the English government itself had become convinced that the destruction of the *Emden* had, after all, not been accomplished. So another order to cancel all sailings was issued. There was, therefore, no reason for the *Emden* to remain in these waters any longer. So our commander decided to devote this interim of enforced idleness to giving the *Emden* the attention that her long continued cruise had made very necessary. The ship's bottom was especially in need of a cleaning. So we turned her nose to the south.

CHAPTER 4

The Flying Dutchman

We knew quite well that sixteen hostile ships were in pursuit of us,—British, French, and Japanese. We never had any information with regard to the position of these ships, nor of their character, which, after all, could matter very little to us, since the *Emden* was the smallest and least formidable of all the war ships in the Indian Ocean. There was not a hostile cruiser, that she was likely to meet, that was not her superior in strength. That the *Emden's* career must soon be cut short was therefore a prospect of which everyone aboard her felt certain. Many hounds are certain death to the hare.

Even should the inevitable encounter be with a hostile cruiser that was not much more powerful than the *Emden* herself, she would nevertheless sustain injuries, and the ship's personnel suffer loss sufficient to oblige us to abandon our present activity. There was not a port where we could put in to make repairs, and vacancies that might occur in the personnel could not be filled in any case. Our commander had set this aspect of affairs before us, sharply and clearly, at the very outset of the *Emden's* career, pointing out that the only future ahead of the *Emden* was to inflict as much damage as possible upon the enemy before she herself should be destroyed, which, in any event, could be but a question of time.

That our foes were always round about us, and at times very near, we learned from the wireless messages which they were constantly exchanging. Although these gave us no definite information, as they were in secret code, they nevertheless revealed to us, by their greater or less distinctness, the distance between us and the ship that was sending the messages. This, to be sure, was no great gain, as the enemy might be in any direction from us. A manoeuvre on our part, for the purpose of avoiding the enemy, could be to little purpose therefore.

By such an attempt we might, instead of eluding the foe, have run straight into the enemy's arms.

It has been frequently said by the English that it was wholly due to her great speed that the *Emden* remained afloat as long as she did. This is not the case. Aside from the fact that the ship's bottom was so heavy with barnacles, etc., that the *Emden* could not run at her highest speed, she could at no time make more than eleven nautical miles on an average, for the very good reason that the coal tenders, upon which she was dependent for fuel, could travel no faster. Moreover, a greater speed would have profited us little. Whereas, at a speed of eleven miles, we found it possible to avoid a hostile encounter, we might, by the greater rate of twenty miles an hour, have rushed straight upon the enemy.

However, the wireless messages we caught up, as we came near to a hostile ship, did tell us something,—they revealed to us the nationality of the ship that was sending them. For there was a distinguishable difference between the wireless messages sent by the ships of our various foes,—those sent by the English were unlike the French, and these, in turn, differed from the Japanese or Russian, if, indeed, the latter ever got so far as to use a wireless apparatus at all.

During these days of raiding, our life on board ship was much as it had been in times of peace. Undoubtedly there were a few more lookouts on duty at night, and, of course, guns and torpedoes were ready for use at a moment's notice, both by day and by night. The *Emden's'* commander spent most of his time on the bridge, where comfortable chairs had been placed for his convenience, so that he could sleep there, and be ready instantly for any emergency. His days were chiefly devoted to the study of marine charts, sailors' handbooks, and other like sources of information. In long hours of careful preparation the plans were here developed that, when carried out, resulted in the *Emden's* remarkable achievements.

The devotion of the *Emden's* crew to their commander was touching in the extreme. The men appreciated the high qualities of their leader, were proud of their ship, and gloried in its successful career. If, at any time when they were singing, or were otherwise noisy, the word was passed along, "The commander is tired," they would become instantly quiet. At a word of encouragement from him the men would accomplish some truly wonderful feats in connection with difficult undertakings, such as coaling at sea under most adverse conditions, and in spite of extreme fatigue. Many a time, while making the rounds of the ship, I have heard them talking about their "Captain," and the tenor of their conversation was usually expressed in a final remark, such as, "Yes, our Commander is fine at it!"

In the officers' mess, also, life went on much as it did in days of peace. To be sure, the comfortable and cosy appearance of the rooms was a thing of the past. All woodwork had been removed, and everything of inflammable material, such as curtains, and the like, had been banished. Ammunition was constantly being transported through the mess, and other work of a like nature was going on there, both by day and by night. The gun that had been mounted in the officers' living room had to be kept in readiness for use at any moment. The officers who were not on duty, and therefore at a particular station, slept in hammocks up on the poop when the weather was fair, or, if it rained, they occupied mattresses or hammocks in the officers' mess, all of them together. To undress was a luxury in which we no longer indulged. Everyone had to be ready to get to his post at a moment's notice.

The pleasantest hours of our life on board were always those spent in reading the newspapers taken from captured steamers. They were the bridge that spanned the gulf that yawned between us and the rest of the world. Even though all the news we received came through the medium of the British press, nevertheless we managed to extract some semblance of truth from out the network of lies, more especially so after we had had a longer experience with the reports sent out by the Reuter News Agency. For instance, we found it very reassuring to discover, by consulting the map, that the "*retreat* of the Germans from France," which the Agency had declared to amount "almost to a rout," had proceeded in a *westerly* direction. Nor did we allow ourselves to be much disturbed by the fact that when we added up the amazing figures that announced the German losses, their total amounted to considerably more than the entire population of Germany.

To the newspapers of India we were indebted also for information concerning the *Emden's* achievements, and we were astonished at the way in which they regarded the whole matter. They seemed to look at it wholly as though it were a kind of sport we were engaged in,—poked fun at their own war ships which, in spite of their numbers, had failed to capture the *Emden*, spoke of our bombardment of the Madras oil tanks as though it were a huge joke, made our commander an honorary member of the principal club of Calcutta, and indulged in a large number of "*Emden* yarns." These were of so absurd a character

THE *EMDEN*

that no one would have thought of offering them, as actual occurrences, to any reading public except one of as little judgment in such matters as the English are. It will be illuminating to quote one or two typical ones as examples.

An Indian newspaper published the story told by the captain of a merchantman, who claimed to have met the *Emden* without having been captured by her. That any faith was placed in even so much of the story is in itself evidence of the credulity of the British reading public, for the captain of an English steamer that came in contact with the *Emden* never got away with his ship. The captain's story was as follows:—

> It was at night, and I was steering toward the Sandhead lightship, but failed to find it where I looked for it. Before long, however, I saw the pilot boat, which threw her searchlight on us. (I must explain that the pilot steamers of this region are, as a rule, equipped with searchlights for the purpose of attracting incoming vessels to themselves.) I steered my ship in the direction of the pilot boat, but was surprised to find that the distance between us did not diminish, and that the pilot, instead of approaching, was running away from me. I ordered my engineer to drive the fires to the limit, and to work the engine at maximum speed. In spite of all this, the difference between us remained the same. I puzzled my brain over this unusual conduct on the part of the pilot.
>
> Before I could arrive at any conclusion, however, and to my utter amazement, the supposed pilot began to navigate in circles, small at first, but growing larger and larger all the time. Like mad I raced after her, and tried to overtake her by steering a short cut on a chord of the circle. The signal I sounded with my steam whistle remained unnoticed. I failed to overtake the pilot boat. After a half hour's mad chase after her, the pilot steamer stopped playing her searchlight, and left me staring foolishly into the darkness. Later, I learned that the supposed pilot steamer was none other than the *Emden*.

This was the captain's story. Angelic simplicity!

Another "*Emden* yarn" was printed by a Calcutta newspaper, and was to this effect:—

> One day an urgent wireless message was received by the government authorities, saying that an English cruiser, coming

from Singapore, had met the *Emden*, and in the pursuit of her had used up every bit of coal in the bunkers, and was now keeping her engines going by burning all available material, such as beds, wardrobes, furniture of every kind, etc., in her endeavour to reach a port on the coast of India. She urgently asked that several thousand tons of coal be forwarded immediately to the port she hoped to reach. The devoted and energetic government authorities at once undertook vigorous measures to comply with the request, and then sent the message on to the next government station, with the order to pass it along.

In their eagerness to participate in anything that might promote the interests of the government, the officials at this second station sent the message on to the next one, where those in charge, also filled with a desire to do something, decided to give immediate orders to a coal company, which, in the meantime, had been swamped with orders from all the stations where the message had been previously received. Eager to make the most of this unusual opportunity for business, the coal company set to work at once' to accomplish something. Hundreds and hundreds of coolies were hired; mountains of coal were loaded into cars that were quickly procured.

Day and night the work went on without intermission. In the shortest time possible train after train, piled high with the much desired black diamonds, was rolling away, at the enormous speed of forty kilometres (about twenty-five miles) an hour, toward the port where the cruiser was expected to put in. Here, also, eager preparations were in progress, so that the cruiser might coal as quickly as possible. No time must be lost in the endeavour to catch the *Emden*. To the great surprise—and delight—of the *coolies*, to the equal degree of astonishment, but less delight, of the railroad officials, harbour master, and residents of the port, and to the utter chagrin of the coal company and the government authorities, no British cruiser put in an appearance.

After a while, this mixed-up state of affairs began to clear. The Indian government had discovered the key to the situation. The wireless message must have come from the *Emden!* How she could have managed to send it in the English secret code, in which the telegram was worded, the British government failed to explain to the credulous public.

Of "*Emden* yarns" such as these there was an untold number. On board ship we kept a scrap-book in which they were all preserved, but this, unfortunately, was lost, together with much that was of higher value.

Amusement of a different nature was afforded the officers' mess by our "war cats," as we called them. On the day before we left Tsingtao a cat had come on board, and so had come along with us. In course of time, this cat experienced the joys of motherhood. Lying in my hammock one morning, I opened my eyes upon a charming scene of family life. Just beneath me, a little to one side, on a mattress on the floor of the deck, lay Lieutenant Schall, sleeping the sleep of the just. Close beside him, on the same mattress, lay the cat, with a family of five newly born kittens. After I had quickly wakened the other officers who were sleeping near, so that they might enjoy the sight of this peaceful domesticity, we poked Lieutenant Schall until he, too, opened his eyes upon the scene. At first he did not seem to share our pleasure in it, however, but, with a muttered oath, hurried off to the washroom.

In conformity to the laws that decide nationality, the war kittens were declared to belong to our mess. In a vacant corner, where a sofa had once stood, we set up a little wooden house, and made a bed in it for the cat and her kittens. Thanks to the devoted care of all the ship's officers and the men who served them, the kittens prospered wonderfully. The instinct by which they were prevented from killing themselves with overeating roused our admiration. In a short time the tiny creatures were able to venture upon short excursions away from their bed. Thereafter, all of us, when moving about the mess, picked our steps most cautiously, because the kittens were always most likely to be just where we were about to place our feet. There was special need of this precaution at night.

When this consideration for our little guests had reached a point where it threatened to interfere with certain nightly manoeuvres, the cat house was placed within an enclosure. Later, when the tiny things had developed into cunning creatures, they used to scamper about on our afternoon coffee table, where they engaged in the most amusing wrestling matches. To knock over the pictures on my writing desk, and to investigate the contents of my waste basket formed some of their chief amusement.

So that we might be able to distinguish them, one from the other, we tied different coloured ribbons around their necks. One day we decided that they must be christened. We named them for the steamers that we had captured. So we had a little Pontoporros, a small Lovat-Indus, and a little Cabigna and King Lud capering about on our table. Only for the last and tiniest kitten did we find it difficult to select a suitable name. It was the weakling of the family, for in its physical development it had remained far behind its brothers and sisters. Its small fragile body was supported on four tottering spindle legs, and it had an astonishingly big head, from which two great, round eyes looked foolishly out upon the world. So we thought that the next name in order, which happened to be *The Diplomat*, was hardly appropriate. But it received a most fitting name from one of the lieutenants, who always referred to it as "the little idiot."

The kittens were often up on the poop, frolicking in the sunshine. At such times all the officers, who happened to be off duty, devoted themselves to nursemaid service, in order to prevent the kittens from falling overboard. Nevertheless, one day the little idiot succeeded in eluding our watchful care. When we assembled at the table for our afternoon coffee, the kitten was missing, and could not be found in spite of diligent search for it. The officers who had been on kitten-watch duty earnestly assured us that the missing one could not possibly have tumbled overboard. But it was gone, and was nowhere to be found. Deep despondency reigned as a consequence of the kitten's loss, but this quickly gave place to loud rejoicing when, in the course of the nightly round of the ship, inspection of the rear 10.5-cm, ammunition magazine revealed the little idiot sleeping peacefully on one of the cases of ammunition. It had got down there by a leap from the poop through the ammunition shaft, a descent of about nine metres. For human creatures of the kitten's tender age we should not advise so daring an undertaking. The little idiot, however, was not much the worse for it. He was lame in one of his hind legs for a few days, and then all was well with him again.

Our kittens were not the only animals that the war had brought aboard our ship. If someone had dropped from the sky, and landed on the *Emden* on one of these days, he would have opened his eyes in wonderment at sight of this "man-of-war." Forward, in the vicinity of the drain pipe, he would have discovered one or two pigs, grunting with satisfaction. Nearby, he would have seen a couple of lambs and a sheep or two, bleating peacefully. By a walk aft he would, in all probability, have scared up a whole flock of pigeons that had been sitting on the rails which served for the transportation of ammunition, and that, at his approach, would take refuge in the pigeon house that had been fastened against one of the funnels.

In his further progress he would most likely have frightened up a few dozen hens that would then have run cackling about his heels, the noise they made being only outdone by the still louder cackling of a flock of geese engaged in unsuccessful attempts at swimming in a large half-tub aft, and at the same time trying to drink salt water. We always had a great deal of live stock on board, all of which we had taken from the captured steamers, and which lent variety to our table. We had a less practical, but more ornamental addition to our menagerie in a dwarf antelope, which I came upon one day in the forward battery. How the dainty creature got there has always remained a mystery to me.

All our animals received devoted care from the men of the crew. Indeed, I cannot suppress a suspicion that the pigs were so assiduously fed with all remnants left from our own meals, in the secret hope that this would hasten the day when they would be served up for our dinners.

The men had much leisure. Under existing circumstances no regular drills, such as are customary in time of peace, could be undertaken. A large part of the crew was necessarily constantly on duty, in service at the engines, or elsewhere in the ship, each man ready at his post. The rest of the men had to be kept in good physical condition, so as to be able to meet any sudden emergency which the war might bring about. In fair weather the men slept at their stations, ready for action with the guns. It was especially desirable to provide comfortable and airy sleeping places for the men who served in the engine room. Oftentimes the rooms provided for this purpose were rendered unfit for occupation by the extreme heat of the tropical climate. A part of deck was therefore set aside as a sleeping place for the men, and provision made for the hanging of their hammocks there. Anyone stepping out upon this deck on a fair night would have seen a "sleeping host" suspended in hammocks, all gently swaying with the motion of the ship.

A part of the day was often devoted to giving the crew a report or explanation of the existing war situation, in so far as this was possible. Oftentimes the newspapers were read aloud, and many of the books belonging to the officers found their way forward, to help pass the time pleasantly for the men.

To keep them informed with regard to the progress of the war was a duty which I reserved for myself. A large map of Germany and the adjacent countries was drawn, and on it the course of events on land was traced.

It was not an easy matter for me to decide just how to handle the subject of the war in my talks to the crew. My only sources of information with regard to it were the English newspapers, which, as is notorious, habitually published the most absurd misrepresentations of what had occurred. Constant annihilation of the German armies, utter disorganization everywhere, complete collapse, starvation, revolution, epidemic of suicide among German army corps commanders were common items of daily news. Great headlines announced that the emperor had been wounded, the crown prince had fallen, Bavaria had withdrawn from the Empire, and other like nonsense.

One course that was open to me in dealing with these newspaper eccentricities was to draw my own conclusion from them, and present this to the men, with a total disregard of the most barefaced English lies; for continued bad news from home could not fail, in the end, to affect the spirits of the men. On the other hand, I had every reason to believe that eventually the newspaper reports would reach the men after all. My serving man would most likely find newspapers in my room, and read them. The mess orderlies were present, and therefore within hearing, when the officers read the newspapers, and discussed their contents.

Now, if what I told the crew had been at variance with that which was repeated to them by the orderlies, it could but be expected that the thought would suggest itself to them that I was intentionally representing matters in a favourable light, and that, after all, the outlook for Germany was more serious than I was willing to admit. A misunderstanding such as this had to be avoided at all hazards. So, from the outset, I told the men that I intended to read the newspapers to them, word for word, and then at the close, I would give them my opinion of what had been read.

As an illustration of how much reliance could be placed in the reports of the Reuter Agency, a telegram which we had intercepted early in August, before we had left the Yellow Sea, served my purpose very well. It read:

> Official. The *Emden* sunk in battle with the *Askold*.

There could be no doubt in the minds of my hearers that this was, to say the least, a gross exaggeration, I could therefore use this telegram as a basis for the belief that all the rest of the newspaper information had about as much foundation of truth.

The men were not slow to realize how little faith was to be placed in these English reports.

Great hilarity was caused one day by a map we found in one of the papers, representing Germany after the British lion had divided the spoils. On this map France extended to the Weser and Werra Rivers, and to the Bavarian frontier, Denmark, down to a line drawn through Wismar, Wittenberge, Magdeburg, Hanover, and Bremen; England had swallowed up Oldenburg and Hanover; the country east of the Elbe, including Saxony, had been deivered into the hands of the *Czar*; Bavaria was an independent country; of the German Empire there was nothing left except a little spot called "Thüringen."

Henceforth the Bavarians and Thüringians among us carried their heads very high,—the former, because their homeland had been recognized even by the enemy as being an essential element, and the latter, because theirs seemed to be regarded as the nucleus of the Empire.

What sport we made of it!

The men always looked forward with eagerness to the time for reading the newspapers. As soon as the papers found on a captured ship had been brought aboard the *Emden*, all eyes asked an unuttered question—"When is the reading to come off?" On such occasions disputes, otherwise unheard of, were likely to arise among the men of the crew as to whose turn it was to be on duty, for no one wanted to miss the reading. Whenever the whistle shrilled out the call: "All hands to the forecastle," it was invariably greeted with an inarticulate yell of delight that rang aft from the forward part of the ship.

Then, after the newspapers had been read, and as clear a portrayal as possible had been given of the most recent events of the war, there were always many questions asked with regard to one point or another.

The chief interest was ever in the ships of the squadron. The victory of Santa Maria, when, for the first time in a hundred years an English squadron had suffered decided defeat at the hands of an equal antagonist, had, naturally enough, roused great enthusiasm. Everyone aboard our ship realized that the fate of all the other ships of the squadron was sealed, quite as well as was that of the *Emden*. For this very reason it gave us all a feeling of satisfaction and pride to know that, before they had met their doom, our armoured cruisers had succeeded in gaining for the Germans the first victory at sea, and in inflicting upon the

English their first naval defeat in a hundred years.

Duty aboard the *Emden* consisted chiefly in keeping the ship itself, the engines, and the armament in condition. To provide a source of refreshment for the crew, a large number of shower baths, made out of old pipes, had been arranged up on deck. The entire crew had a shower bath three times a day, each man being allowed to enjoy it as long as he liked.

The state of health aboard the *Emden* was excellent. From the time we left Tsingtao until the day of our encounter with the *Sidney* there was not a case of sickness on board.

Every afternoon the ship's band gave us quite a long concert. At such times the men all sat cosily about on the forecastle, listening to the music, some joining in with their voices, while others smoked or danced. In the evening, after darkness had set in, the singers aboard usually got together, and then every possible and impossible song was sung by a chorus that was excellent both in volume and quality. The "possible" songs were, to a great extent, our beautiful German national melodies, and these were always well rendered. The "impossible" ones were frequently improvised for the occasion. In these, clearness of enunciation was always a greater feature than either rhyme or rhythm. The singing invariably closed with the "Watch on the Rhine" in which all hands on deck joined.

Distributing the booty we had taken from a captured ship was always an occasion about which centred a great deal of interest. Anything of a useful nature, especially everything in the line of food, was, as a matter of course, taken aboard the *Emden*. As a result, veritable mountains of canned goods were stored away in a place set apart for them on the forward deck. Casks full of delectable things were there. Hams and sausages dangled down from the engine skylight. There were stacks of chocolate and confectionery, and bottles labelled "Claret" and "Cognac," with three stars.

To the accompaniment of a barnyard medley of grunting, squeaking, bleating, and cackling, the different kinds of livestock that were to be entered upon the inventory were driven to the various places prepared for them. The steward stood by with his assistants and entered everything upon his list. When his account was complete, the distribution took place. The men stood lined up in a wide circle, smoking and chatting while they waited, and when they had received their share, they had their hands full for quite a while, as they carried off all the good things, and stored them away in their end of the ship.

So as to be able to do justice to all that fortune bestowed upon us, an extra meal or two had to be tucked in between the usual ones. So, with our afternoon coffee we now had chocolate or *bonbons*. For the smokers there were more than 250,000 cigarettes stored away, and when, in the evening, they had been passed around, the deck looked as though several hundred fireflies were flitting about it. The English flour, which we found in great abundance, kept our bakers busy, with the result that we had most excellent bread. Because of this superabundance of provisions, the chief concern of the responsible officers was to prevent an overfeeding of the men, and not, as in time of peace, to see to it that they were not undernourished.

That many other useful things besides eatables found their way to the *Emden*, it is needless to say. Whenever I went aboard a captured steamer, a list of all the articles desired was always given me. There were but few times when these wishes remained unfulfilled, even when they called for such unusual things as screw-taps, fine or course, soldering lamps, piassava brooms, sheets of rubber, hand vices, bull's-eye lanterns, iron bars, firebricks, machine oil, and the like.

The men I took with me to the captured steamers to carry the things aboard the *Emden*, usually knew just what the men of our crew would like to get of such articles as were to be had, but which did not appear on my list. But all the suggestions that were made to me in this respect could not be carried out. I felt compelled to refuse to allow oil paintings, large mirrors, toy drums, horses, and the like to be taken aboard the *Emden*.'

When we happened to be in a reflective state of mind, we often thought of our pursuers,—how close to us they were all the while, and yet, during their long continuance at sea, compelled to live for weeks on hardtack and corned beef, while beer, wine, cognac, fresh eggs, roast chicken, juicy hams, chocolate, *bonbons* and cigarettes were only phantoms of the imagination to them, seen in teasing dreams, or remembered as the delights of their last visit ashore.

So we spent the passing days, while certain death lurked round about us. In sixteen ships our enemies were burning their coal, and racking their brains in vain attempt to catch us.

As there was not a merchantman of the enemy now abroad, our commander, as has been related, decided to give the *Emden* a much needed overhauling, especially to clean the bottom of the ship. So we steered a southerly course, which took us out of the Bay of Bengal, and, one fine morning, our anchor rattled down into the sea for the first time in many a long day. We were in the harbour of Diego Garcia, a small island belonging to England, and situated in the extreme southern part of the Indian Ocean.

Hardly had we anchored when the English flag was joyfully run up on shore. A boat with an old Englishman in it put off from the island and came toward us. With his face beaming with the pleasure of seeing someone from the outside world, he came on board, bringing with him gifts of fresh eggs, vegetables, etc. He gave eager expression to the delight it afforded him to have the opportunity, after many years, once more to greet some of his German cousins, so dear to his heart, and so highly esteemed. He assured us that he was always so glad to see the Germans, especially those that came in their fine war ships. He had not seen one of them since 1889, when the two frigates, the *Bismarck* and the *Marie*, had run into the harbour. That was a long time ago, he remarked, but for this very reason it made him all the happier to see us now, and he hoped it would not be long before another German ship would anchor at Diego Garcia.

At first we were somewhat surprised at this greeting, although by this time we had become accustomed to all kinds of English eccentricities. But soon we learned from our guest that Diego Garcia receives a mail only twice a year, by way of Mauritius, and so the people on the little island as yet knew nothing of the war. We surely were not disposed to acquaint them with the horrors of existing conditions. Why should we? And, moreover, it might so happen that we would come again before many days had passed.

However, when our guest came on board the *Emden*, and, looking about him, saw the condition of this German man-of-war, he opened his eyes wide in astonishment. Instead of the usual white deck, shining with cleanliness, he beheld an ill-looking, oil-stained flooring, blackened by coal dust, and furrowed with deep scratches. He saw that the colour of the engine skylight was more nearly black than gray, that the railing was not only broken, but entirely missing in places, that only small patches of linoleum were still to be seen here and there, that thickly plaited matting was hung about the guns as a protection against splintering, that there were many spots on the walls indicating that something was gone that had either stood or hung there, and that in the officers' mess there was a remarkable scarcity of furniture.

When he beheld all this, he was blank with astonishment, and wanted to know what it all meant. We tried to reassure him, however, by telling him that we were on a cruise around the world, that this made it desirable for us to dispense with everything that was not absolutely necessary, and that we had to use every available place for coal. In addition, we treated him so generously with whiskey, that presently he gave up thinking at all. He did not seem to find this a very difficult thing to do. With an effort, he managed to ask us to do him a favour, which was that we should repair his motor boat for him, that he had not been able to use for the past half year. This we promised to do, and we kept our word.

We made the most of the time we spent in this quiet and remote harbour to put our ship in as good condition as possible, to give her a thorough cleaning, and especially to scrape the bottom, and give it a fresh coat of paint. The latter could, of course, be only imperfectly accomplished, and was managed by letting water enough into one side of the ship to give it a slanting position. Men in small boats then cleaned and painted as much of the bottom as had been raised out of the water in this way.

While we lay in the harbour, we found diversion in a novel sort of hunting. Looking down from the deck one day, we saw two objects floating in the water close by the ship. At first sight we took them to be bundles of dirty rags that had been thrown overboard. Suddenly, however, we saw that the objects moved, and were silvery white on the underside. Upon closer inspection they turned out to be two enormous rays. I estimated their size to be from four to five square metres. They had great wide, shiny yellow mouths, which they opened to catch the small fish they were chasing.

Rifles were quickly brought out, and we tried to get a shot at the creatures. To do this, we had to wait for the propitious moment when they raised their backs somewhat out of the water. One of our shots, fired at just the right moment, hit one of the fish squarely on the back. Tossing and splashing, it made a leap from twenty to thirty centimetres high out of the water, all the while flapping violently with its broad fins, causing a commotion in the water resembling that produced by the beating of the wings of a large bird.

Much to our disappointment, we failed to secure the fish however.

Naturally, some of the time we passed in the harbour was devoted to fishing. Everywhere out of the side windows dangled fish lines, and the efforts of the fishermen brought rich reward. The queerest specimens were pulled up. Fish of every colour were there,—red, green, and blue ones; broad fish, and narrow, pointed ones; some with eyes on their upper side, while others had them underneath, and still others were provided with long spines. They were all landed on deck, but were not allowed to be eaten until the ship's doctor had examined them and pronounced them fit for food, as we were aware that certain kinds of fish are poisonous.

We saw sea snakes also. But, to our regret, we failed to catch any. They were about two metres long, and light green in colour. The creatures had a peculiar way of leaping upward out of the water, all the while whipping vigorously back and forth with their tails, assuming an almost vertical position as they moved rapidly along on the surface of the water.

This idyll of southern seas could, unfortunately, be of but short duration. Soon the *Emden* was on her way to new fields of action. In the vicinity of Minikoi Island we captured a great many more prizes, for, by this time, shipping had ventured forth once more.

We were especially pleased that the British Admiralty again saw fit to send us a fine steamer of 7000 tonnage, carrying a cargo of the best Welsh coal. But, before long, no ships were to be seen in the neighbourhood of Minikoi Island. Either all shipping was again being kept at home, or else a different course was being followed. It behooved us therefore to discover the route by which the steamers were now going.

First of all, we searched the water to the north of Minikoi Island. And behold, in the shortest possible time we came upon an English steamer, whose captain, when he was captured, exclaimed in great surprise: "Tell me, how did you learn of the new and secret course laid out for merchantmen by the Admiralty?" That was hint enough for us, and we forthwith looked for more ships in this region. And we did well to do so.

As a result, we renewed our acquaintance with an English lady whom we had met before. I noticed at once how calmly she accepted her unusual situation. She went about the deck with great composure, distributing chocolate and cigarettes among our men. From her conversation it soon developed that she had grown quite accustomed to having her plans interrupted by the *Emden*. First of all, while on her way from Hong Kong to Europe, the ship on which she was travelling had turned back while still in the Yellow Sea upon learning that the *Emden* was near.

After that, the lady had spent several weeks idly waiting in Hong Kong. Then she had managed to get as far as Singapore, from whence she had started out afresh, and again she had the experience of having her ship called back to the harbour from which she had sailed, because it was reported that the *Emden* was in the neighbourhood. After a few more weeks of waiting, this time at Singapore, she had got as far as Colombo, and on her way out from there she had met the *Emden* after all Her return trip to India was made on one of our junkmen.

To capture steamers at night was no easy task for the *Emden*, and always made great demands on our men. We could never be sure whether or not it was a man-of-war we were approaching. Therefore, whenever we did not know, beyond a peradventure, that it was a merchantman, the men were summoned to their battle posts. Furthermore, we had to reckon with the possibility that the English would protect their merchantmen by a convoy of war ships. In that case the latter would follow at a short distance behind the ships they were escorting, and, when the *Emden* attention was fixed upon the steamer she was raiding, an unexpected attack would be made upon her.

On one occasion, we thought that we had surely run upon a man-of-war. The night was black. Ahead, and coming toward us, we saw a steamer that was showing lights, apparently a merchantman. The *Emden*, with screened lights, of course, ran toward her on a course at an angle with her own. Just as we were about to turn on our lights, to give chase, we saw a large dark object close behind the steamer. We thought it might be a man-of-war travelling without lights. As we could not make out what it was, we prepared for any event. So the order was: "Both engines at full speed, straight away! Torpedoes ready! And at her!"

Upon closer approach it developed that our fierce attack was being made upon nothing more dangerous than a heavy cloud of smoke that the steamer had just belched forth, and which, owing to the absence of wind, lay upon the water in the steamer's wake.

Unfortunately, we found it impossible to avoid running upon neutrals in this particular vicinity, and these, after an inspection, had to be allowed to proceed. Without a single exception they were Dutch ships.

However, our experience with them was happier than the one we had had with the *Loredano*. Not once did we intercept a wireless message in which the Dutch made any allusion to the *Emden*. On the other hand, we ourselves could not hope to get any news of the war from these ships, as the Dutch government, in the endeavour to preserve a strict neutrality, had forbidden the transmission by wireless of any information with regard to the war. We caught up one message, sent by an English to a Dutch ship, asking for news of the war. The answer was:

> We are not allowed to transmit war news of any kind.

Thus, within a comparatively small expanse of the sea, the *Emden* continued to do her part in the great war, constantly pursued by sixteen hostile war ships, and, of course, compelled to remain close to the usual steamship routes, as there only could we hope to secure any prizes.

That, in spite of this, we managed to elude our enemies, together with the fact that the *Emden* appeared, like a will-o-the-wisp, first in one quarter, and then in another, gave rise to the assumption by the English papers of India, that there were a number of German raiders abroad, and that they all had adopted the name *Emden* as a ruse. Indeed, in course of time we ceased to be called the *Emden* at all, and were generally known as *the flying Dutchman.*

Chapter 5

Our Baptism by Fire

Again there was a total absence of merchantmen, and, as the *Emden* had just been put into good condition, some new and profitable service must be found for her. Her commander had come to the conclusion that, besides Colombo and Singapore, the enemy must be using still another base for taking on coal and provisions, and for recuperation. The port which suggested itself as the one most likely to be serving this purpose was Penang. We had gathered from newspaper reports that the French armoured cruisers, *Montcalm* and *Dupleix*, frequently put into port there. To attack these or any other ships that might be lying in the harbour was the task which our commander now set himself.

On the night from the twenty-seventh to the twenty-eighth of October the *Emden* arrived at a point just outside of Penang, and was approaching the harbour at full speed. It was her commander's intention to run in as soon as the day dawned. The narrow entrance to the harbour offered too many difficulties to make it advisable to attempt it by night. Moreover, it is in the early hours of the coming day that human weariness is most likely to assert itself, and so make the prospect of success by surprise more hopeful.

Aboard the *Emden* all hands were waked bright and early. The ship was cleared for action to the utmost, that is, everything was put in a state of absolute readiness for battle. A hot and hearty breakfast was served to the men. Clean underclothing and fresh suits were put on, to lessen, in so far as possible, all danger of infection in case of wounds.

Without a light showing, nor a bit of smoke escaping, and with every man at his post, the *Emden* drew near to the enemy's port. It was just before sunrise. The night was dark. But in these southern latitudes the full light of day bursts suddenly upon the world with the rising of the sun. Here and there, in the darkness of the night, we passed a lone fishing boat lying near the entrance to the harbour, one or two of which we would have run down had it not been for the watchful eye of the officer on duty, who managed to steer clear of them.

Close to the entrance of the harbour we saw, to port of us, a bright white light that appeared and disappeared with lightning-like rapidity, remaining in sight only a couple of seconds at a time. Beyond a doubt it was an electric light, and was therefore, apparently, some sort of outpost or sentinel vessel. We felt quite sure of this, although we did not catch sight of the ship itself. The fact that it was here indicated the presence of war ships in the harbour.

On the *Emden* the fourth funnel, which had done us good service on many a former occasion, had of course again been set up.

Just as our ship had reached the inner roadstead of Penang, the first darting rays of the coming day flashed into the sky. We had arrived at just the right moment. During the brief and quickly passing dusk of dawn we discovered a large number of ships lying in the harbour. Apparently they were all merchantmen. The closest scrutiny failed to reveal anything that looked like a man-of-war. We were just beginning to think that this time we had made a mistake, when suddenly, in the midst of all the merchantmen that were showing lights, we saw a dark object on which there was not a light to be seen. It had every appearance of being a war ship. In a few minutes we had come close enough to see that, beyond doubt, it was some kind of war craft. Then suddenly, on this dark and suspicious looking object, there appeared three lights at equal distances from each other. Our first thought was: Those are the stern lights of three destroyers that are lying side by side.

But soon we realized that this could not be the case. The hull of the vessel that was now getting more and more distinctly visible was evidently too large to be that of a destroyer. Unfortunately, the ship in which we were so interested was lying in the current, which brought her stern pointing toward us, and we could not, therefore, get a side view of her. Not until the *Emden* had approached to a distance of not more than two hundred metres, had passed by and taken a position to the one side of her, did we recognize the *Schemstchuk*.

On board, peace and quiet reigned. All hands were sleeping strenuously. We crept so close up to her that even in the prevailing dusk of the early morning the Russian cruiser was easily recognized. Not an officer on duty, not a watch on the lookout, not a man of the signal service was to be seen. We sent our first torpedo whizzing over to her from our starboard broadside tube, while at the same time our broadside poured shells into the forepart of the *Schemtschuk*, where the crew was sleeping. Our torpedo hit the enemy's cruiser aft. The jar which shook the ship as our torpedo struck was plainly visible. There was a slight upward movement of the after part of the ship,—from about a quarter to a half metre high,—and then the stern slowly settled.

Now matters began to look lively on the Russian. The doors leading on to the deck from the officers' rooms were torn open. A large number of the officers came running out, but did not seem to have a very definite idea of where their battle stations were, for, without any further ado, most of them ran as far aft as the flagstaff, and then promptly jumped over- board. They were followed by a whole company of sailors,—evidently the sort of fellows who do not hesitate to go through thick and thin with their masters. Meanwhile our rapid gun fire, delivered at close range, was doing devastating work on the *Schemtschuk*.

At a distance of four hundred metres, and very slowly, the *Emden* passed by the hostile cruiser from stern to bow, pouring broadsides into her all the while. Before many minutes had passed the fore part of the ship looked like a sieve. Smouldering fires were eating their way through the interior of the ship. Great holes in both sides of the hull made it possible to look clean through the ship. Clap upon clap the shells struck. When they hit, there was a bright, sharp flash. Then, for the space of a few seconds, fiery rings seemed to be rapidly circling around the spot where the shell had struck, until, almost immediately afterward, masses of black smoke from the interior burst forth through the great holes in the sides of the doomed ship. We did not see a man leave the fore part of the *Schemtschuk*.

Meanwhile, the *Emden* was being fired upon from three sides. Where the shots came from, we did not know. We could only hear the whistling of the shells, and see them fall on the merchantmen that lay on every side of us. The *Schemtschuk* now also took a hand in the game, and began to fire at us. As her guns were of greater calibre than our own, their shells, if they had struck the *Emden*, would have proved disastrous to her. Even had our ship not been disabled, the dam- age sustained would in all probability have been sufficient to make it impossible for us to continue our present activity, as the *Emden* had no port of refuge where she could make repairs. Our commander therefore gave orders to fire another torpedo.

In the meantime the *Emden* had passed beyond the *Schemtschuk*, had turned hard about to port, and was passing by her opponent for the second time. When the distance between the two ships had been reduced to four hundred metres, our second torpedo went flying over to the *Schemtschuk*.

It had grown so light in the meantime that we could plainly see the whirling course of the missile as it sped on its way. In a few seconds there was a terrible explosion on the Russian cruiser, in the vicinity of the pilot bridge, A great thick cloud of black smoke, mixed with grey, and shot through with white steam and spray, rose to a height of one hundred and fifty metres, or more. Loose parts of the ship went flying up into the air. We could see the cruiser break apart in the middle, while bow and stern dipped into the water at the same time. Then the cloud raised by the explosion hid everything from sight, and when, in about ten or fifteen seconds, it had cleared away, there was nothing to be seen of the cruiser except the truck of the mast head protruding out of the water.

Quantities of debris, and many men swimming about in the water marked the spot where the ship had disappeared. It was not necessary that we, of the *Emden*, should rescue the survivors of the *Schemtschuk*, as there were numbers of fishing boats near, which immediately went to their assistance.

All shooting had ceased by this time. Our other two antagonists that, in addition to the *Schemtschuk*, had fired upon us, had also discontinued their fire. Moreover, we did not know just where the shots had come from.

Suddenly, lying at anchor among the merchantmen, and half hidden from our view by them, we discovered the French gunboat *D'Iberville*. It must have been from her that some of the shots fired at us had come. Our commander had just ordered the *Emden* to turn to port, and, passing by the wreck of the *Schemtschuk*, to go to the attack of the *D'Iberville*, when the lookout at the mast head reported a hostile destroyer running into the harbour from out at sea. This was an enemy it would not be safe for us to meet here in the narrow entrance to the harbour, as it would be quite impossible for us to execute any manoeuvre by which we could avoid the torpedoes that would be fired at us.

Our commander decided therefore to run out toward the destroyer at the top notch of our speed, so as to meet her in the broader expanse of the outer harbour. We saw the ship very plainly as we approached each other. There was the high, pointed forecastle with the low, wide funnel behind it, and a course at high speed directly toward us,—the typical appearance of one of the large English destroyers.

At a distance of 4000 metres our first shot went whizzing over to her. All around her we could see high columns of water raised by the shells as they struck the sea. Hereupon, the vessel quickly turned hard about to starboard. It was then that we discovered that she was only an English Government steamer of medium size. It was due to the refraction of the rays of light which is so common in tropical regions, and especially at sunrise, that the ship's outlines had been so distorted as to lend her the appearance of a destroyer. We ceased firing.

But again, just as we were about to turn and get after the *D'Iberville* for the second time, there came a report from the lookout announcing that another large ship had been sighted running into the harbour. While we were still at a great distance from her, it was plainly to be seen that this time we were dealing with a merchantman. Our commander determined first of all to make sure of this latest arrival. The *D'Iberville* could not get away. Our cutter was rushed down to the water. We gave the steamer the usual signal: "Stop! We are sending a boat." But hardly had our cutter arrived alongside the ship when again a war vessel of some kind was seen approaching through the entrance of the harbour. So the cutter was quickly recalled and hoisted aboard, and then we drove toward this latest comer.

The illusions due to refraction were most unusual on this morning. Every few minutes the outlines of the approaching ship seemed to change. At first she appeared to be a large black ship with funnels fore and aft. Beyond a doubt, therefore, this must be a man-of-war. Then suddenly her dimensions shrank together. Half of the funnels we had seen, disappeared altogether, and she now looked like a merchantman, painted gray, and with black bands around the funnels. Only a few minutes later the vessel had changed her appearance again. She had grown smaller, was black, and had two funnels. From this we concluded that she must surely be a French torpedo boat destroyer. So, at her at once!

The *Emden* was not flying her flag at the time, nor was the ship that was approaching showing her colours. When about 6000 metres distant from us, she ran up the tri-colour. A Frenchman, therefore! She was coming at us at right angles to our course, and apparently did not know just what to make of us. By what the Frenchman's attitude was determined is a mystery to me. Our shots and the detonation of the bursting torpedoes must have been heard afar, and one would suppose that any cruiser leaving the harbour immediately afterward would have been viewed with suspicion, to say the least. Nevertheless, the ship kept on her course toward us. When we had reached the 4000 metre range for our shots, up went, our battle flags. The *Emden* turned easily to port, presented her broadside to the enemy, and our first shot went humming over to her.

Now the Frenchman realized who we were. She turned hard about to port, put on all steam, and tried to run away from us. It was too late. The *Emden's* third salvo had lodged five shells astern in her opponent. A detonation followed, apparently an explosion of ammunition; then a great cloud of black coal dust, mingled with white steam, shrouded the whole stern end of the fleeing ship. It must be conceded that, in spite of the hopelessness of their position, the Frenchmen set vigorously to work to defend their ship. They shot two torpedoes at the *Emden*, and the forward guns of the destroyer opened fire upon us. The torpedoes failed of their mark, however, for the *Emden* maintained a distance beyond the range of a torpedo. They dropped into the water about 900 metres off from our starboard side. Nor did the Frenchman's guns continue their fire long, for soon they were silenced by the hail of shells we fired into the destroyer. Mast, funnel, forward tower, superstructure, ventilators,—everything on the Frenchman was shot away. In a few minutes more the ship had sunk. It was the French destroyer, *Mousquet*.

The *Emden* now steered for the spot where her foe had disappeared in the sea. Both cutters were lowered for the purpose of picking up the survivors who had come to the surface of the water. They were floating about, clinging to drifting spars, or kept afloat by life-preservers, and were scattered along a considerable distance,—an evidence that some of the men must have jumped overboard at the very beginning of the engagement. The *Emden's* cutters were provided with dressing for wounds, in so far as this was possible, and carried the ship's doctors.

As our cutters approached the Frenchmen, who were swimming all about us, a strange thing happened. Instead of striving to reach our boats, they made every effort to get away from us. Yet the distance to the nearest shore was so great that the swimmers could not hope to reach it through their own efforts. The reason why they sought to get away from our boats was not revealed to us until later. We picked up thirty-three Frenchmen, some of them wounded, and one wounded officer. Thanks to the precaution we had taken in sending doctors out with the cutters, two-thirds of the wounded arrived on board our ship resting in transport hammocks, with their wounds dressed, and their limbs in splints, where these were necessary.

In the meantime a second French torpedo boat was seen steaming out of the harbour and heading for us. For the *Emden* it was now high time to be gone. In all probability there were more French and English warships in the neighbourhood. An encounter by daylight with a superior force of the enemy must be avoided by the *Emden*, dependent, as she was, upon herself alone. So we headed for the open sea, and kept a westward course at high speed. The French torpedo boat chaser followed us for a while, but ran into a squall of rain, in which she disappeared, and was not seen again. Thus our purpose to entice the Frenchman out to sea, and then turn and destroy her, came to nought. Our French prisoners, both the wounded and the well, were comfortably provided for on the *Emden*. All who were suffering from injuries found rest and care in the ship's hospital.

For those who had escaped injury an ample and firmly constructed shelter house, built of boards arid sail-cloth, was put up on the starboard side of the middle deck, near the engine skylight. In our crew were two sailors who spoke French fluently. These two men were now excused from all other duty, and acted as interpreters for the wounded in the hospital, and for the other Frenchmen as well. Benches and tables for the use of our prisoners were quickly put together. The Frenchmen, most of whom had no suits on when they came aboard the *Emden*, were not only willingly, but cheerfully provided with clothing by our men, although their own supply was getting very low. The prisoners received plenty to eat and to drink, and were provided with something to smoke. In their liberty of action they were as little constrained as possible.

When I asked some of the Frenchmen why they had swum away from our cutters that were out to rescue them, they replied:

"The reports in our newspapers have always been that the Germans massacre all prisoners, and our officers confirmed these statements. We preferred drowning to being butchered."

When, in further conversation, we asked why they had allowed the *Emden* to get away on the night we ran out of the harbour of Penang, their answer was that although they had seen the *Emden* very well, they had taken her to be the English cruiser *Yarmouth,* and so had allowed her to go on her way undisturbed. It is most likely, therefore, that the white light we saw on the night at Penang was this French torpedo boat destroyer. The Frenchmen also told us that their commander had both his legs shot off by one of our shells; that he might have been saved, but refused, and, tying himself fast to the bridge, went down with his ship. He did not want to survive the shame of seeing some of his men jump overboard in an effort to save themselves at the very beginning of the fight. Hats off to such an officer! Among the wounded were three whose injuries were of so severe a nature that nothing could be done to save them. Of these, one died on the first evening after the fight, and the other two on the following day.

According to the custom among sailors, the body of the first one of these prisoners to die was sewed up in sail-cloth and weighted at the feet. It was then carried to the starboard deck aft, placed on a bier, and draped with the French war flag. A guard kept watch beside the bier throughout the night. The services for the dead took place on the following morning. At these ceremonies a company of the *Emden's* men, dressed in their parade suits, was present. All the unwounded Frenchmen also were allowed to participate. A guard of honour, carrying arms, and in command of an officer, was stationed at the bier. All the German officers, in uniform and wearing their decorations of honour, were in attendance.

Our commander gave a brief address in French; in it he paid tribute to the dead as having given his life for his country, by which he had earned the honour and respect of friend and foe alike. The service ended with a prayer rendered in accord with the dead man's religious belief, and read from a Catholic prayer book. Wrapped in the French flag, the dead was then committed to the sea from the stern gangway ladder. The ship's engine was stopped for the occasion, and the guard of honour fired three volleys with due ceremony over the Frenchman's last resting place. The *Emden's* officers stood at salute beside the gangway ladder. Like solemn ceremonies took place on the following day when the other two Frenchmen, who had died, were consigned to their watery grave.

Within a few days our French prisoners were all transferred to an English steamer that was carrying a neutral cargo, the destruction of which would have been to no purpose. When they were told that they were going to be sent off, the two senior non-commissioned officers among them asked to be allowed to speak to the *Emden*'s commander. To him they expressed their gratitude, as well as that of their comrades, for the kind and humane treatment and comfortable shelter they had received aboard our ship. To this they added that they now knew that what their newspapers had said of the Germans was all lies, and that on their return to their native land they would do all in their power to make the truth known. The two officers expressed like sentiments to me.

Before leaving us, the French officer who was so seriously wounded asked for an *Emden* cap band, saying that he wanted very much to have a memento of the ship whose officers and crew had treated a vanquished foe with so much chivalry, and the wounded with so much kindliness.

Quantities of the *Emden's* surgeon's supplies were sent over to the steamer, to be used in dressing the wounds of the injured Frenchmen, The captain of the steamer was then directed on his way to Sabang, where he was advised to take the wounded, as the nearest hospital was to be found there. To our regret we learned from the newspapers, some time afterward, that the wounded officer had died there.

The English gave the most absurd account of this fight at Penang. They stated that only by flying the English flag had the *Emden* succeeded in getting into the harbour unrecognized, and further, that she had entered the harbour from the south, and had left it by the north passage. These are all inventions, and are utterly false. In the first place, at no time did the *Emden* ever fly the English flag, nor would it have been to any purpose to have done so in this instance, for we ran into the harbour at night. Furthermore, the south entrance to Penang harbour is too shallow to allow the *Emden* to pass through it at any time.

The only words of the English report which I can confirm are those of commendation for our commander, with which it concludes the description of the sinking of the *Mousquet*, and the rescue of the survivors. The words are these:—

> Here we have another instance of that chivalry which the *Emden's* commander has so often shown in his meteor-like career during this war. Every minute was of incalculable importance to him, as at any moment other French torpedo boats might have come out to attack him. But, with no thought of the danger he was incurring, he stopped his ship and sent boats out to pick up the survivors of the *Mousquet*, before proceeding on his way. As the saying goes, *He played the game.*

In addition, I wish to express my agreement with the following words of the report:

> So ended the battle that will live in history as evidence that two ships of about equal fighting strength can engage each other at shortest range imaginable without the inevitable destruction of both. An incident such as that which occurred yesterday has been declared by most naval authorities to be impossible, or at least suicidal

The man who made the report evidently had little acquaintance with men such as the *Emden's* commander.

Chapter 6
Our Daily Bread

How to provide our ship with coal was a question of vital importance to us. On our course from Tsingtao southward and into the Indian Ocean we were attended by our faithful companion, the coal tender *Markomannia.* But her supply had nearly come to an end when we arrived in the Indian Ocean. There was no harbour to which we could go for coal. So we had to earn "our daily bread."

To be sure, we had been so fortunate as to capture, for our first prize, the coal steamer *Pontoporros,* which had aboard several thousand tons of coal for us. But, as has been said, this coal was of so inferior a quality that it could be of use to us only in case of extreme need. We did burn the *Pontoporros's* coal for a short time, but, whenever we did so, a tall, telltale column of black smoke rose above our ship; the fire kettles became clogged, and lost in capacity; the entire deck was always covered with a layer of fine bits of coal and cinders; through every crack and every window penetrated the smeary black coal dust. In short, every man of us longed for better fuel to burn. Our joy at capturing a cargo of several thousand tons of first-class Welsh coal was greater than if it had been a steamer laden with gold.

The *Emden* coaled very frequently. For the event of an engagement with the enemy it was necessary always to have a large quantity of coal on hand. At no time, therefore, could we allow our store of fuel to fall below a certain minimum. Consequently, the taking on of coal was as essential to us as was our daily bread.

For the crew, it was neither an easy nor a pleasant job,—this constant filling up with coal. The heat of the tropical climate was intense. This was most noticeable in the bunkers, where the coal had to be trimmed, and where the temperature often rose to a point that was almost unendurable. To be sure, while employed at coaling, the men wore hardly any clothing at all. Their "little coaling packs," as they dubbed them, which consisted of an old and otherwise useless suit of clothes, fit only for the work of taking on coal, had suffered severely in the continuous use to which they had been put in this everlasting coaling. We could not afford to sacrifice any of the better suits of clothes to this dirty work. So the trousers that had originally been long ones soon became ragged below the knees, and were shortened to knee pants. After a while these were reduced to the length of bathing trousers, and still later—but the less said of them in this stage of their existence, the better. Moreover, a thick coat of coal dust took the place of anything else that may have been lacking.

We had to coal at sea. Now, in the Indian Ocean there is always a rather heavy swell, by which ships are kept in constant motion. There were times, therefore, when we ran considerable risk in taking on coal.

To protect a ship when going alongside of another, fenders are used. They are either large mats, or balls made of cordage or of reedwork, and are placed so as to prevent the two ships from grinding, or being damaged by the impact. The fenders we carried with us were soon worn to shreds by the lively antics that the *Emden* and her coaling steamer usually carried on. It soon became evident, also, that they were by no means large enough to insure protection during the strenuous business of coaling at sea. It behooved us, therefore, to get to work at making new ones.

Before we left Tsingtao I had taken the precaution to purchase one hundred and fifty hammocks. My original intention was to make use of them in case of leakage. Hammocks can be very effectively used, when a ship has suffered damage below the water line, by stuffing them into the leak, whereby the amount of water that forces its way in is lessened.

These hammocks now stood us in good stead. We constructed large and long fenders out of logs, from four to six metres in length, by covering them with a thick layer of hammocks. When needed, these fenders were hung along the sides of the ship. To be sure, they were always much the worse for wear when we were through with the coaling, but before they were needed again, we could make new ones.

We had still another novel sort of fender, the like of which, I dare say, had never before been used. On one of the steamers we had captured, we found a large number of automobile tyres. Everywhere along the sides of the ship we hung these elastic rings, and they made most excellent buffers.

The task of coaling at sea was necessarily a long and tedious process. Oftentimes the two ships that had been lashed together rolled badly. In that case, when the bags of coal on the coaling steamer had been hoisted up on the boom, the favourable moment had to be awaited when the two ships rolled against each other; then the braces were quickly eased, and the coal went plunging down somewhere on to the *Emden's* deck. It then behooved the men to jump away from the coiling as nimbly as possible, and get out from under.

That the constant grinding of the ships against each other, and the continuous plunging of the heavy bags of coal down upon the *Emden's* deck resulted in all manner of damage to the ship, can be readily imagined. The *Emden* carried a gun in each one of her "swallow's nests" (side structures), fore and aft. Now, when the ships rolled against each other, the forward "swallow's nest" was always in imminent peril, and was on several occasions severely damaged. The chief sighting mechanism of a cannon is always placed on its left-hand side. Therefore, by coaling on the starboard side of the ship the possibility of damaging this chief sight was avoided. And indeed the auxiliary sighting mechanism, which is on the right-hand side of the gun, was crushed in before many days of coaling had passed. The doors of the "swallow's nest" had given way on one occasion when the coaling steamer had lurched against the *Emden*, and, being forced inward, had struck against the gun.

The bags of coal often caught in the railing. Ere long there was not an undamaged railing post on the entire starboard side. The linoleum deck also suffered greatly. Soon it was worn through. There were large holes in it, which laid bare the polished steel deck beneath. This, in itself, was of little consequence, but the places where the steel was exposed were so smooth that, especially at night, and when the ship rolled badly, the men often slipped on it, and fell. For this reason, as soon as we had finished coaling, men were set to work at roughening the steel surface wherever it was exposed. To this end we used chisels, with which we cut narrow grooves into the steel, thereby giving the men a firmer hold for their feet. Somewhat later, after one of the English steamers had provided us with a large quantity of tar and some very strong sail-cloth, we covered the deck with this,

For the *Emden*, as has been said, it was absolutely essential that she should be well provided with coal. For this reason we not only packed the bunkers to their full capacity, but stored quantities of coal on deck.

Forward on the forecastle, in the middle near the engine skylight, and aft on the poop, great heaps of coal were piled. Naturally, this greatly interfered with the passage way from one part of the deck to another. Oftentimes, while moving about on deck, we had to wind our way in and out between piles of coal that rose to a man's height. Occasionally, when the ship rolled heavily, the coal would slide, whereby the deck would be rendered impassable for a time.

Coal dust and dirt were everywhere. So long as there was any coal still stored somewhere on deck, the first duty of the morning, as soon as all hands were up, was to move some of this coal from the deck into the bunkers, to replace that which had been consumed during the last twenty-four hours. The wood of the deck suffered severely from this constant dragging of heavy sacks of coal over it. Deep black furrows were worn into it. There were oil spots to be seen everywhere. That the paint on every part of the ship grew dirty and grimy needs not to be mentioned. No one, seeing the *Emden* as she now looked, would have recognized in her the trim ship that, on account of an always scrupulously correct appearance, was called the *Swan of the East*.

Our antagonists have always held that coaling at sea is not feasible under any circumstances. In coming to this conclusion they probably gauged the difficulties of the undertaking by the capability of their own crews. We found that the enemy was always looking for us in every quiet bay and hidden nook that could suggest itself. in connection with coaling, in the supposition that, sooner or later we would have to run into one of these places. Instead of doing so, however, we always coaled at sea.

Even yet I am amused as I recall the amazed and questioning expression on the face of the English captain of our prize, the *Buresk* (he had accepted service with us, as will be remembered) when one day, while there was a heavy sea running, his ship received orders by signal, "Get ready to coal." He thought it was an impossibility, and that it would end in the destruction of both ships. Six or eight hours later, he had to admit that German seamen do not allow themselves to be hindered by swells, or heavy seas in the discharge of their duty.

At best, the transfer of coal always took a long time. Nevertheless, the *Emden* sometimes made a very good record at it. When the weather was unfavourable, we took over about forty tons an hour. But there were times when the weather favoured us. On such occasions we averaged seventy tons an hour. Anyone who has ever undertaken to coal at sea will appreciate that this is good work.

We coaled alternately from the *Buresk* and the *Exford*. Even though the *Emden* by no means escaped injury from the continuous rolling while taking on coal, nevertheless our greatest anxiety was always for the coaling steamers. We feared they might not be able to endure the strain, although they were both very recent products of English shipyards, and were on their maiden voyage. But they were so lightly constructed, and so poorly built that they never got through without receiving great dents in their sides. Poor stuff, they were!

The times when the *Emden* had one of her coal tenders alongside were always hours of danger for us, for the ship could not be in a state of readiness for action at such times. We knew full well that death was lurking at every hand. At any moment an enemy might appear on the horizon and come to attack us. Then there would be much for us to do before we could be ready to meet our foe. While we were coaling, it was absolutely necessary to protect the guns by a close covering. Some of them had to be run in, for while projecting beyond the sides of the ship they were in danger of being damaged. It was highly advisable for us, therefore, to coal as speedily as possible. The men realized this fully, and always did their utmost.

Oh the other hand, everything was done to make this necessarily strenuous labour as light as possible. At such times the steward always prepared an abundance of lemonade, which was poured into great half-tubs and set in readiness in the forward part of the ship. This drink was made more refreshing by the addition of ice. Cans and cans full of the cold lemonade were passed to the men who were at work. The ship's band played lively airs the while, to cheer them. A large slate was set up somewhere near the middle of the ship, where it could be easily seen by everyone, and on it the progress made in coaling was recorded. At the end of every quarter of an hour the number of tons taken aboard appeared on the slate in large figures written with white chalk. The amount accomplished by each watch was scored separately. The men of one watch were eager not to allow themselves to be outdone by the others. With great interest, therefore, every higher record made by the one group was noted by the men of the other, and when their turn came, strenuous efforts were made to surpass it.

Aloft in the tops sat the lookouts, provided with glasses, and faithfully searched the horizon with keen eyes for the least indication of a suspicious looking mast head, or speck of smoke.

When the transfer of coal had progressed far enough to allow the coal tender to pull off, there was still much to be done aboard the

Emden. First of all, the coal on the deck had to be piled into place; when so much was done, at least the greater part of the dirt had to be removed from our sleeping places. Then the men had to wash, get under the shower baths, and put on clean clothes. After that came supper, and then,—to sleep in the hammocks. Often enough, however, the weary men had scarcely got to rest when a steamer would appear in sight, and they would be summoned to renewed exertion. It would then be hours before they could get to rest.

Truly, the life we led was not one of case! But the thought that it might be otherwise never suggested itself to any one of us. On one occasion, on a night when the men had gone to rest after they had been strenuously at work for ten hours, our commander, at my suggestion, allowed a steamer to pass unmolested, because I told him that the men appeared to have reached the limit of their strength. When, on the following morning, the men learned of this, a murmur of disapproval arose among them. "We could have finished that one too," they growled.

Chapter 7

Distress of the Nibelungs

Upon leaving Penang our commander decided to run farther to the south for a while. It was to be expected that all shipping would be kept out of the Bay of Bengal for some time. Had not the *Emden* given indisputable evidence of her presence in these waters by the destruction of the *Schemtschuk* and the *Mousquet?* In all likelihood the search for the *Emden* in the Bay of Bengal would be more vigorously pushed now than ever before. On the other hand, the waters in the vicinity of Sunda Strait offered a more promising prospect as a hunting ground for the enemy's merchantmen. Ships of commerce coming from Australia hardly get into the Bay of Bengal at all, but strike a course from Sunda Strait, or from West Australia directly across the ocean to Socotra, and thence into the Red Sea.

The first thing for us to do now was to look up our coaling steamer *Buresk,* which had been dismissed just before we got into Penang harbour. With a speed limit of barely eleven miles, the tender was not a desirable companion during an engagement.

Without delay we found the *Buresk* at the appointed place. The account of our successful exploit was received aboard the *Buresk* with great enthusiasm. The two ships now proceeded southward at their usual speed of eleven miles. Soon the Dutch islands lying along the west coast of Sumatra came in sight. As merchant ships usually follow a route that takes them between these islands and the main coast of Sumatra, our commander chose the narrow water ways of this region for his next sphere of action. Moreover, as the water is much more quiet between these islands than it is out at sea, it would be much easier to coal there. Furthermore, it was our opinion that these quiet waters were most likely to be frequented by Japanese and English torpedo boat destroyers. It was not improbable, therefore, that we might catch one or two of them there.

While we were in the vicinity of the island of Sima-loer it was again time for the *Emden* to take on coal. The sea was very smooth, and so the task was quickly accomplished. Our ship lay at a distance of about eight nautical miles off shore, and quite beyond the limits of neutral waters therefore.

Nevertheless, after a little while, a fishing boat propelled by motor was seen coming toward us. The Dutch flag was flying at her mast head. She brought a Dutch official, who came aboard the *Emden* and introduced himself as the commandant of the island, and asked if we were not within the limit of territorial waters. If this was the case, he must request us to go farther out to sea, he said.

Whether this was the real purpose of his coming, or whether he merely wished to have a little chat with us, I cannot say. A mere glance at the distance must have told him that we were considerably more than three nautical miles away from the shore. He remained with us for a while, and was invited into the presence of our commander.

From this Dutch official we learned that Portugal had declared war against Germany. This afforded us considerable merriment. We always enjoyed a joke.

At the very beginning of our acquaintance I had unintentionally offended the commandant of the island. As he came alongside in his boat, I mistook him for a fisherman, and asked if he had any fish to sell. To this he replied by an indignant negative. However, this little misunderstanding did not affect our further acquaintance, and he seemed to feel very much at home in our mess.

For a while, the *Emden* continued to cruise about in the vicinity of Sunda Strait. But not a ship came in sight. Evidently all traffic in this region had been discontinued. Ordinarily there is a great deal coming and going through Sunda Strait.

It had now been fully two months that our ship had been beating about in the midst of her many foes. As has already been said, every man aboard the *Emden* was fully aware that she could not continue her activity indefinitely, and that sooner or later she must meet disaster. Conditions were steadily growing less favourable for us. When we first entered the Bay of Bengal we could count with certainty upon the circumstance that our enemies were not anticipating anything so audacious. For a while, therefore, we had little to fear from warships, as there were hardly any in the Indian Ocean. Most of them were probably in the Pacific, engaged in the pursuit of our armoured cruisers.

Soon, however, we learned from newspaper reports, and other sources of information, that a considerable number of war ships, superior to our own, were searching for us. Much of this information we got from the crews of the prizes we took.

We naturally supposed that England would follow her usual tactics of misrepresentation, and that therefore the people of India would be utterly deceived with regard to the true state of affairs. And so it was, for at first all the English-speaking Hindoos taken from the captured steamers had but one story to tell,—continuous German defeats. Later, however, there was a change of tone. One native of India, with whom we talked toward the end of September, said that English newspapers declared that Germany was defeated. Now, however, many newspapers of India pictured conditions very differently. But these papers were suppressed by the English, he said. Nevertheless, most of the men of India felt convinced that matters were not proceeding as favourably for the English as they would have the world believe. It was his opinion, moreover, that "England by and by finished."

Another Hindoo related a peculiar incident. He told us that two English cruisers, having each two masts and two funnels, had for some time been held in the harbour of Colombo. While one of the two cruisers was doing guard duty out at sea, the other one remained in the harbour. At stated intervals the ships relieved each other, the one in the harbour going out to take the place of the one at sea. One day the cruiser that had been out at sea returned with only one funnel and one mast, badly battered up by shells, and with many wounded on board. From that day forth the second cruiser was not seen again. This may have been one of the many times when the *Emden* was destroyed.

A Chinaman coming from Hong Kong related that two Japanese cruisers, badly damaged and with many wounded on board, had run into Hong Kong one day.

The *Emden* had no share in this fight, nor, as we now know, did any of the other ships of the German squadron take part in it.

All things considered, there was every reason to believe that the *Emden* was being vigorously pursued. The day when her career must come to an end could not, therefore, be far distant. The men aboard her did not allow this prospect to dampen their spirits, however. When the fateful moment had arrived, the enemy should be made to realize that in the *Emden* he had met a worthy foe.

As not a ship made its appearance in the Sunda Strait, our commander decided to find employment in destroying the wireless and cable station on Keeling Island. Telegraphic communication between Australia and the motherland had already suffered considerably at the hands of the other ships of our squadron. The station at Keeling afforded the last opportunity for direct communication between Australia and England. Should this also be disabled, the only remaining connections would be by means of the neutral Dutch cables, *via* the East Indies. We naturally assumed, therefore, that the English had taken every precaution to defend this, the last station remaining to them. It would have been an easy matter for them to station a hundred men at Keeling for its defence, and so render futile any attack by a landing squad from the *Emden*.

In that case there would be nothing that the *Emden* could do but to shell the station, and inflict as much damage as possible in this way. It would not amount to much, however. The cables, in particular, would remain intact, and for all the smaller necessary apparatus on shore there were probably duplicate parts in reserve, by the use of which the station could be put into running order only a few hours after the bombardment had ceased. The English had reason to believe also that if the island was effectively garrisoned, the *Emden* would refrain altogether from shelling the station. It would be the part of wisdom for the *Emden's* commander to be sparing of his ammunition, and it was not at all probable that he would use it for the purpose of temporarily crippling the telegraph service.

As there was sufficient reason, therefore, to expect a vigorous defence of the island, all necessary measures were taken to render the proposed landing expedition as effective as possible. The four machine guns which the *Emden* carried were taken along. A squad of fifty men was mustered. In addition to the machine guns the men took with them twenty-nine rifles and twenty-four revolvers. More than fifty men could not be spared from the *Emden* for landing purposes. Her crew was too small. Our three prizes, the *Pontoporros*, *Exford*, and *Buresk* had all been manned from the *Emden's* crew, besides which a few of our men had been needed on the *Markomannia*.

On the night from the eighth to the ninth of November, 1914, the *Emden* and her tender, the *Buresk*, lay fifty nautical miles to the west of Keeling. The coal tender *Exford* had been sent to a given point of meeting farther out at sea. It was quite possible that we would find some English cruisers lying at anchor in Keeling harbour. In that case the *Buresk* would, most likely, be discovered and captured, while the

Emden, in the hope of being able to continue her activity for a while longer, would seek to avoid the encounter with a greatly superior foe; She could then find her other coaling steamer somewhere out of sight of the enemy.

That night the *Buresk* received orders to remain at a certain point, fifty nautical miles to westward of the island, and not to proceed to Keeling until ordered by wireless to do so. After accomplishing the destruction of the station, our Commander intended, if everything went smoothly, to coal in Keeling harbour.

At sunrise, on the morning of the ninth day of November, the *Emden* lay just outside the entrance to Port Refuge, the anchorage for Keeling Island. The way into the harbour was a rather difficult one, as it led in and out among the reefs; but we found it, and the *Emden* dropped anchor. The landing squad was ready and waiting. The men got into the boats at once, and put off for the shore at just half-past six in the morning. They landed without encountering resistance of any kind.

In two hours the work on shore was done. The landing squad was just about to re-embark when the *Emden* signalled by searchlight: "Hurry your work." Almost immediately after the signal had been given, the *Emden* sounded her siren. This meant danger. Our men of the landing squad saw the *Emden* suddenly weigh anchor, turn, and run out of the harbour. The attempt made by our boats to overtake their ship by striking the shortest course toward her, although it led directly across the reef, proved of no avail. Soon afterward the *Emden* ran up her battle flags, and opened fire upon an enemy not visible to the men in the boats. Great water spouts, caused by the plunging of shells into the sea close to the *Emden,* gave unmistakable evidence that an enemy, though unseen, was near.

Ashore on Keeling Island, and unable to do the least thing to help their ship and their comrades, our men of the landing squad beheld with bitterness the unequal fight that now ensued.

The *Emden's* antagonist was the Anglo-Australian cruiser *Sidney.* She was half again as large as the *Emden,* built five years later, was her superior in speed, protected by side armour, which the *Emden* was not, was equipped with guns that, although in number no more to the broadside than the *Emden* carried, were of a calibre that was one and a half times as great,—conditions under which there could be but one outcome of the battle. For the *Emden* the hour of destiny had struck.

Soon the two ships were engaged in a running fight, all the while

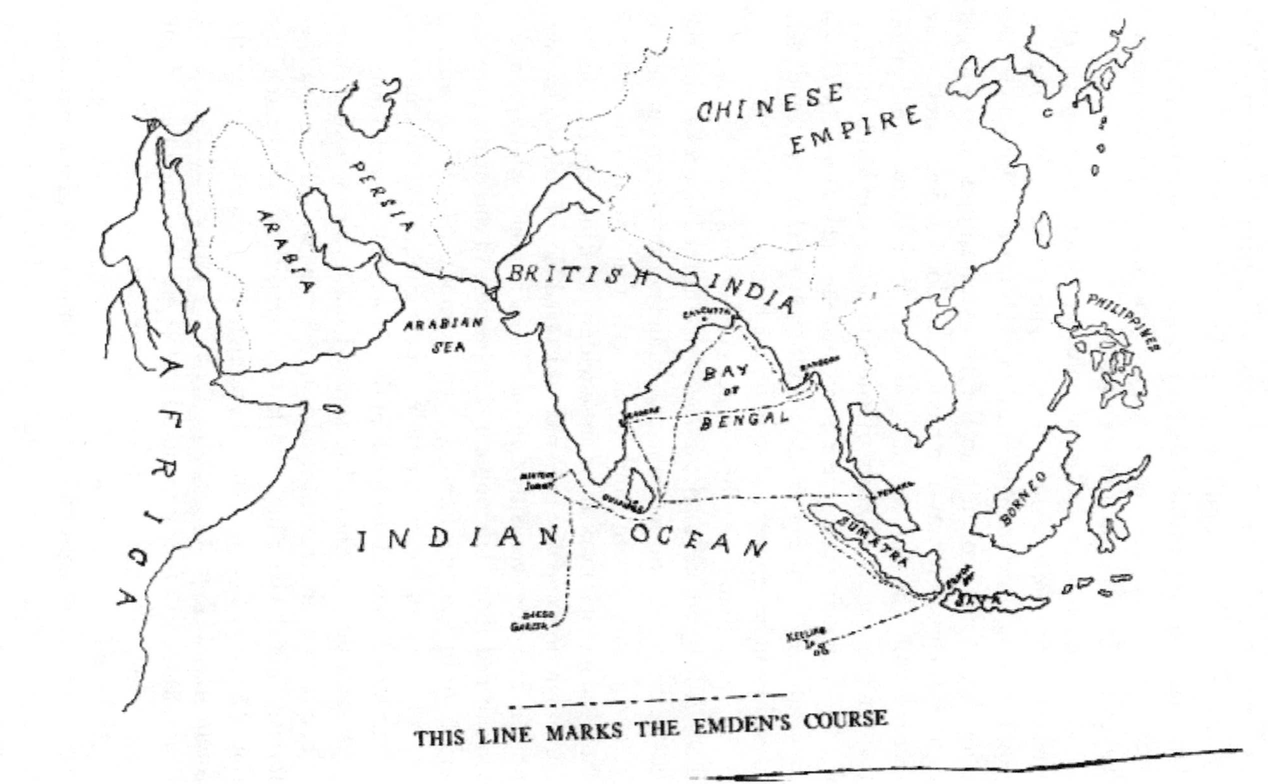

THIS LINE MARKS THE EMDEN'S COURSE

keeping at a distance of from four to five thousand metres from each other. From ship to ship sped the iron missiles in full broadsides. At the outset it appeared that the enemy was suffering considerably. The *Emden's* first salvos found their mark forward in the hostile cruiser. The marksmanship of the English was not much to boast of. For a time, not a telling shot had struck the *Emden*, although our gunners had given a good account of themselves.

But after a while, a well-placed salvo struck aft on the *Emden*. The havoc that the *Sidney's* shells of great calibre wrought on our unarmoured cruiser was tremendous. A great blaze started up under the poop. For a quarter of an hour the flames leaped upward to a height of from twenty to twenty-five metres. The cloud of dense grey smoke that rose from the ship was mingled with white steam, an indication that the steam pipes on the starboard side of the ship had been damaged. Undaunted by the severe injury that she had suffered, the *Emden* now squarely faced her assailant. Putting her helm hard about, she turned upon her enemy and took up the battle.

Unintermittently the forward guns of our ship poured forth their shells. A few minutes after the *Emden* had turned upon her foe, the hostile cruiser also turned to starboard, and ran away from our ship. As in the meantime we on shore had observed that several of the *Emden's* shots had hit their mark, there arose within us a faint hope that the enemy might in some way have received a fatal blow. Evidently this was not the case, however. Although the *Sidney* ran off at high speed, she soon turned about. Undoubtedly the purpose of this manoeuvre was simply to increase her fighting distance from the *Emden*, in order to take advantage of the greater calibre of her guns, and at the same time to put herself beyond the reach of the *Emden's* less powerful guns.

Meanwhile the *Emden* had suffered still further serious damage. While turning about to make a dash at her foe, a shell tore away her forward funnel. Like a huge block it lay across the forward part of the ship. Almost at the same instant another telling shot carried off the foremast, and swept it overboard. When my eyes beheld this, I knew that at least one of my comrades had lost his life,—the officer doing observation duty up in the top of the foremast.

And still the fire continued to rage on board the *Emden*, although it began to show signs of abating. It became more of a smouldering fire, and the flames gave way to a thick cloud of smoke and fumes, apparently the result of efforts to quench the fire. In a running fight, keeping side by side, and firing incessantly with full salvos upon each other, the two contending ships disappeared beyond the horizon.

The fight had begun at half-past eight in the morning. The landing squad from the *Emden*, was now getting the *Ayesha*, an old schooner that they had found lying at anchor in the harbour, ready to put to sea. In case the *Emden* did not return, the men intended to leave the island on this little schooner. During the course of the day the *Emden*, still fighting, came into view a number of times, but always so far distant that she could not be recognized. At intervals the *Sidney's* great cloud of black smoke, due to the Australian coal that she was burning, came in sight. From this, the men of the landing squad knew that the fight was still in progress.

Toward evening, just before darkness set in, the ships came in sight again. They were both still firing. The last that the landing squad saw of the fight was the *Emden* slowly steering an easterly course just before sunset. The ship was almost entirely below the horizon. Only the one funnel still left her, and the top of the highest mast were visible; this was just enough to indicate to us the speed at which she was moving, and the direction in which she was going. The visible distance from Keeling to the horizon is about eight or ten nautical miles.

It is clear, therefore, that shortly before sunset the *Emden* was still afloat, and not more than eight or ten nautical miles distant from South Keeling. The *Sidney* was somewhat nearer to the island. Her masts, funnels, superstructure, and upper deck could all be seen. Both ships were still firing, although the *Emden's* fire was intermittent and not strong. Either her ammunition, upon which the bombardment of Madras and the fight at Penang had made heavy demands, was giving out, or else the majority of her guns had been silenced.

At sunset the *Sidney* ceased firing, and was seen coming back on a north-westerly course. The *Emden* was steering toward the east.

Gradually the distance between the ships grew greater and greater, until at last they were beyond the reach of each other's guns. The fight was over.

The sun set. Darkness fell. Like a black shroud the night settled down upon both ships.

On shore the landing squad was getting ready to leave Keeling on the *Ayesha*, and go in search of the *Emden*.

And so, for nearly ten hours, our ship had maintained an unequal fight against a greatly superior enemy. How great is the advantage of superiority in armour, speed, and calibre can, generally speaking, be appreciated only by those who are familiar with naval affairs.

On land an inferior force, strategically disposed, and taking advantage of local conditions, well ensconced and protected by wire entanglements, with masked batteries and machine guns, can no doubt hold a decidedly superior attacking force at bay for some time, and under most favourable conditions may even prevent the latter from accomplishing its purpose,—for instance, from breaking a way through. Under such circumstances the assailants, even when greatly superior in numbers, cannot gain any special advantage. Superiority in fighting strength is offset by the favourable lay of the land, of which the weaker force can take advantage.

Not so at sea. There is no shelter to be found there. Granted that there is equality of personnel, the battle is decided by the size of the calibre, the quality of the armour, and the degree of speed possible.

When these factors are taken into consideration, the *Emden* did marvellously well. Unarmoured, less speedy, considerably smaller, and carrying much less heavy guns than did her armoured antagonist, she maintained the battle for nearly half a day, until darkness put an end to it.

The men of the landing squad, now aboard the *Ayesha*, saw nothing more of the *Emden*, although they looked for her all through the night. Not until three weeks later, when they arrived at Padang, did they learn what had been the fate of their ship.

The tale is told. The *Emden* is no more. On the rocky reefs of North Keeling she found a grave. But as long as the Monsoon sighs among the tops of the tall pines on the lonely little island in the distant Indian Ocean, and, mingling its voice with the murmur of the shining white surf that breaks on the shore, chants a dirge for the *Emden*, so long shall live, in song and story, the *Flying Dutchman*, the brave little German ship that for months was the terror of her enemies, in 1914, during the great war of the nations, in the mighty struggle for the freedom of the seas.

Ship without harbour, knowing no ease,
Emden, flying over the seas—
German laurel is wound round thy mast,
Curses of England are chasing thee fast;
Ship after ship thou sinkest alone,
And the sea, the sea, the sea is thine own.

Ship without harbour, knowing no ease,
Glorious Emden, pride of the seas—

Thou hast succumbed to an enemy's blow?
Destroyed by flames—the work of the foe?
Thou hast been sunk in the depth of the sea?
Thou—thou art dead? Nay, that never can be!

Ship without harbour, knowing no ease.
Unforgettable queen of the seas!
Emden, thou never, never canst die:
Over the seas thy shadow will fly.
Ever to make the enemy quail.
Ever in German hearts to sail!

Maria Weinand

(English version by Margaret Münsterberg. Poem by Maria Weinand)

The "Ayesha" Being the Adventures of the Landing Squad of the "Emden"

Hellmuth von Mücke

Contents

Translator's Preface

The translator has so enjoyed rendering this little volume into English, that she feels impelled to testify to the pleasure it gave her, and to express a hope that it may find many readers who will follow its record of valiant deeds with as great interest.

That men placed in almost daily peril of their lives can retain their sense of humour and a kindly attitude toward men and circumstances throughout a desperate struggle with adverse conditions is a happy testimony to the buoyancy and to the superiority to the merely physical that courage in the face of danger begets.

Although always bravely confident, there is an engaging ingenuousness and freedom from self-conceit in Lieutenant von Mücke's delightful recital of his amazing achievement, while his never failing appreciation of the humorous side of the situation illumines the entire narrative as with flashes of sunshine.

The translator desires also to acknowledge her indebtedness to an earlier but unpublished translation of the book by Mrs. Anne Richmond Vaughan.

Helene S. White

January, 4th, 1917

Foreword

That *Truth is Stranger Than Fiction* is amply illustrated in the following gripping narrative. I have read practically all the stories and yarns of this war, many in their original languages, but I have found none to surpass this interesting tale. In the years to come, all men, especially those "*who go down to the sea in ships*," will find in these adventures some very profitable lessons in perseverance, resourcefulness and courage. Although this feat may be dimmed by the light of the major operations of the war, I predict that no reader who has once started to read this book will fail to complete it, nor on completion, will he fail to say that he has enjoyed a most interesting series of adventures.

J. H. Klein, Jr.,
Lieutenant, U. S, Navy.

Washington, D. C.
3 January, 1917

Chapter 1

Keeling Island

"I report for duty the landing squad from the ship,—three officers, six petty officers, and forty men strong."

It was on the ninth of November, 1914, at six o'clock in the morning that I reported for duty to the commanding officer of His Majesty's ship, *Emden*, Captain von Mueller, at the gangway of the ship. The *Emden* was lying at anchor in Port Refuge, a harbour formed by Keeling Reefs. Alongside were the two cutters in which the officers and men of the landing squad had already taken their places. The steam launch was ready to push off and tow them ashore. My orders were to destroy the wireless telegraph and cable station on Direction Island, which is the most northerly island of the Keeling group, and to bring back with me, in so far as possible, all signal books, secret code books, and the like.

Three cables run from Direction Island, one line to Mauritius, another to Perth in Australia, and a third to Batavia. As this station was the last absolutely British connection between Australia and the motherland—the other cables having been cut by some of the other ships of our cruising fleet—we had every reason to suppose that we would meet with vigorous military resistance. For this reason we were taking with us all of the four machine guns that the *Emden* carried. Two were aboard the steam launch, the others had been put on the cutters. The men were equipped with rifles, side arms, and pistols. The launch took the cutters in tow, and we were off for Direction Island.

Even quite small boats must pick their way very carefully while within the waters of this atoll[1] in order to avoid the numerous, constantly changing coral reefs. The course that we were to take from

1. Group of coral islands.

the ship to the point at which we were to land, covered a distance of about 3,000 metres.

Direction Island is very flat, and is covered with a luxuriant growth of tall palms. Among their towering tops we could discern the roofs of the European houses and the high tower of the wireless station. This was our objective point, and I gave orders to steer directly for it. Just below our landing place a small white sailing vessel was riding at anchor.

"Shall we destroy that, too?" inquired one of my lieutenants, pointing to the little schooner.

"Certainly," was my answer. "It has sailed on its last voyage. Detail a man at once to be ready with the explosive cartridges."

With our machine guns and firearms ready for action, we landed at a little dock on the beach, without meeting with resistance of any kind, and, falling into step, we promptly proceeded to the wireless station. The destruction of the little white sailboat was deferred for the time being, as I wished first of all to find out how affairs on shore would develop.

We quickly found the telegraph building and the wireless station, took possession of both of them, and so prevented any attempt to send signals. Then I got hold of one of the Englishmen who were swarming about us, and ordered him to summon the director of the station, who soon made his appearance,—a very agreeable and portly gentleman.

"I have orders to destroy the wireless and telegraph station, and I advise you to make no resistance. It will be to your own interest, moreover, to hand over the keys of the several houses at once, as that will relieve me of the necessity of forcing the doors. All firearms in your possession are to be delivered immediately. All Europeans on the island are to assemble in the square in front of the telegraph building."

The director seemed to accept the situation very calmly. He assured me that he had not the least intention of resisting, and then produced a huge bunch of keys from out his pocket, pointed out the houses in which there was electric apparatus of which we had as yet not taken possession, and finished with the remark: "And now, please accept my congratulations."

"Congratulations! Well, what for?" I asked with some surprise.

"The Iron Cross has been conferred on you. We learned of it from the Reuter telegram that has just been sent on."

We now set to work to tear down the wireless tower. The men

in charge of the torpedoes quickly set them in place. The stays that supported the tower were demolished first, and then the tower itself was brought down and chopped into kindling wood. In the telegraph rooms the Morse machines were still ticking busily. What the messages were we could not decipher, for they were all in secret code. But we chuckled with both amusement and satisfaction as we pictured to ourselves the astonishment of the senders, who were waiting in vain for a reply to their messages, for, from the vigorous action of the apparatus, we concluded that some information was eagerly desired. But this, to our regret, it was not in our power to furnish.

Our next duty was quite to the taste of my vigorous boys in blue. A couple of heavy axes were soon found, and, in a few minutes, Morse apparatus, ink bottles, table legs, cable ends, and the like were flying about the room. "Do the work thoroughly!" had been our orders. Every nook and corner were searched for reserve apparatus and other like matter, and everything that bore any semblance of usefulness in a wireless station was soon destroyed. Unfortunately this fate was shared by a seismometer that had been set up on the island. In their zeal my men had mistaken it for a lately invented addition to the telegraph service.

To locate and cut the submarine cables was the most difficult part of our task. A chart, showing the directions in which the cables extended, was not to be found in the station, but close to the shore we discovered a number of signboards bearing the inscription, "Cables." This, therefore, must be the place where we must search for the ends of the cable strands. Back and forth the steam launch carried us over the cables that were plainly to be seen in the clear water as we tried to grasp them with a couple of drags and heavy dredging hooks, which we drew along the bottom. It was no light task, for the cables were very heavy, and the only power at our command was a very limited amount of human strength. For a while, it seemed impossible to draw the cables to the surface; in the end, after we had succeeded in raising the bight of the cable a little, my men had to get into the water, dive, and tie tackle to it, by the aid of which we continued our labour.

With great difficulty we at length succeeded in getting the cable strands into the boat. I did not want to use any of the dynamite cartridges for the work of destruction, as the *Emden* might have need of them for the sinking of more steamers. So we set to work upon the stout cables with crowbars, axes, driving chisels, and other like implements. After long and weary labour, we succeeded in cutting through two of them, and we then dragged the ends out to sea, and dropped them there. The third cable was not to be found in spite of our diligent search for it.

A small house of corrugated iron, in which were stored quantities of reserve apparatus and all sorts of duplicate parts, was blown up and set on fire with a couple of explosive cartridges. All newspapers, books, Morse tapes, and the like, we took away with us.

Our landing squad was just about to re-embark when, from the *Emden*, came the signal "Hurry your work." I quickly summoned my men, abandoned my intention of blowing up the small white schooner as a matter of little importance, and was on the point of pushing off from shore, when it was reported to me: "The *Emden* has just sounded her siren." This was the command to return to the ship with the utmost despatch. As I was boarding the steam launch, I saw that the anchor flag of the *Emden* was flying at half mast, which told us that she was weighing anchor. The reason for this great haste was a mystery to me, and, for the present, was no concern of mine. All my effort was bent upon getting back to the ship as speedily as possible. With all steam on we raced toward the *Emden*, taking the shortest course between the reefs.

Meanwhile, the *Emden* had turned seaward, and was running at high speed out of the harbour. My first thought was that she was going to meet our tender, the *Buresk*. that had been ordered here with coal, and which, I supposed, she was going to pilot through the reefs. In this belief I continued to follow the *Emden* as fast as I could, but was surprised to find her going at a speed of from sixteen to seventeen miles. Our launch, with the heavily laden cutters in tow, could make barely four miles an hour.

Suddenly we saw the battle flags on the *Emden* run up, and then a broadside burst from her starboard. Even yet the reason for all this was hidden from me, and I believed the *Emden* to be in pursuit of a steamer that had come in view.

But now a salvo of five heavy shells struck the water just aft of the *Emden* ; five tall waterspouts marked the places where they fell into the sea. There was no longer any room for doubt; we knew that a battle was on in earnest. The *Emden's* opponent we could not see, for the island, with its tall palms, was between us. The *Emden*, in the meantime, had increased her distance from us to several thousand metres, and was adding to her speed with every moment. All hope of overtaking her had therefore to be abandoned, and I turned back.

CHAPTER 2

The "Ayesha"

We landed at the same place at which we had gone ashore before. Again I ordered all the Englishmen to assemble, and their firearms were taken from them. The German flag was raised on the island, which was declared to be under martial law; every attempt to communicate by signal with any other island, or with the enemy's ships, was forbidden; my officers were given orders to clear the beach for defence, to mount the machine guns, and to prepare to intrench. Should the engagement between the two ships prove to be a short one, I could count with certainty upon the enemy's cruiser running into port here, if for no other reason than to look after the station. It was not my intention, however, to surrender without a blow an island on which the German flag was flying.

The Englishmen on the island were little pleased at the prospect, and begged permission, in case it should come to a battle, to withdraw to one of the other islands. Their request was granted.

Accompanied by two of my signal men, I now took my station on the roof of the highest house to watch the fight between the two cruisers. As a whole, the Englishmen showed little interest in the conflict that was going on but a few thousand metres distant from the island. Other matters seemed to claim their attention. With an ingratiating smile one of them stepped up to our officers, who were head over ears inwork down on the beach, and asked:

"Do you play tennis?"

It was an invitation which, under the circumstances, we felt compelled to decline.

By the time I had reached the roof, the fight between the *Emden* and the other cruiser was well under way. I could not identify the enemy's ship, but, judging from her structure, and the amount of water raised by the falling shells, I concluded that it must be one of the two Australian cruisers, the *Sydney* or the *Melbourne*. As the columns of water raised by the enemy's shells were much taller than those caused by the *Emden's*, I estimated the guns of the enemy to be of 15 centimetre calibre.

The *Sydney*, for she it was, as I learned later, was more than a match for the *Emden*. Our ship of 3,600 tons displacement could deliver a broadside of only five 10½ centimetre guns, and had no side armour, whereas the *Sydney*, being a vessel of 5,700 tons displacement, could fire a broadside of five 15.2 centimetre guns, and had armoured sides. From the very beginning, the *Emden's* fire reached its mark on the enemy's cruiser, whose guns, it must be said, were aimed pretty badly. The water spouts that were raised by their falling shells were mostly several hundred metres distant from one another. But when one of the volleys did hit, it made havoc on our unarmoured vessel.

During the very first of the fight, the forward smoke stack of the *Emden* was shot away and lay directly across the deck. Another shell crashed into the stern aft of the cabin, and started a great blaze, the gray smoke of which was mixed with white steam, showing that the steam pipes had been damaged. The *Emden* now turned sharply about and made a dash for her foe, apparently for the purpose of making a torpedo attack. It cost her her foremast, which was shot away and fell overboard. For the moment it seemed as though the enemy's ship intended to discontinue the fight, for she turned and ran at high speed, followed by the *Emden*. Whether the *Sydney* had suffered serious damage which could not be discerned from without, I could not tell. Perhaps it was simply her intention to increase her fighting distance from the *Emden*, in order to take advantage of the greater calibre of her guns.

The running fight between the two ships now took a northerly course at an ever increasing distance from the island, and soon the two cruisers, still fighting, were lost to view beyond the horizon.

The point for me to settle now was what to do with the landing squad. So far as our ship was concerned, the damage she had suffered at the hands of a far superior foe was so great that a return to the island, even in the event of a most favourable outcome of the battle, was out of the question. She must run for the nearest port where she could make repairs, bury her dead, and leave her wounded. At the same time I could count with certainty upon the arrival of an English war vessel ere long in Keeling harbour, to learn what had befallen the cable and wireless station. For, had not the telegraphic service to Australia, Batavia and Mauritius been cut off entirely?

With our four machine guns and twenty nine rifles we could, for the time at least, have prevented the English from making a landing on the island, but against the fire of the English cruiser's heavy guns, which would then have been directed against us, we would have had no defence whatever. Taking everything into consideration, therefore, we could do no more than defer the surrender of a position that, from the outset, it had been impossible to hold. Moreover, confinement in an English prison was little to our taste.

Now, fortunately for us, the small white schooner that we had failed to blow up was still riding at anchor in the harbour. It could, and it should help us to escape from our predicament. I decided to leave the island on the little boat. Her name was *Ayesha*,[1] and at one time she had served to carry copra from Keeling to Batavia two or three times a year, and to bring provisions back with her on her return trip. Now that steamship service had been established between these two points, she lay idle and dismantled in the harbor, and was gradually falling into decay.

Taking no one with me, I got into the steam launch and went out to the schooner to learn whether she was at all seaworthy. The captain and a single sailor were aboard her. Of the former I inquired casually whether he had any ammunition aboard, for I did not wish him to suspect the real purpose of my coming. He said there was none, and a brief inspection of the ship led me to believe that she was still seaworthy. Consequently I sent my officers and men aboard the *Ayesha* to get her into trim for sailing.

There was plenty to do on the little ship. All the sails and rigging had been taken down and stowed away, and had now to be put in place again.

When the Englishmen on the island realized that it was my intention to sail off in the schooner, they warned me with great earnestness against trusting ourselves to her, saying that the *Ayesha* was old and rotten, and could not stand a sea voyage. Furthermore, they informed me that an English man-of-war, the *Minotaur*, and a Japanese cruiser were in the vicinity of the island, and that we would surely fall a prey to one of them.

As my predecessor in command of the *Ayesha* was leaving her,

1. Ayesha is not an English but an Arabic name, and is pronounced Â-ee-sha. Âyesha is the name of the favourite wife of the Prophet Mohammet.

THE *AYESHA*

he wished us Godspeed, and concluded with the comforting remark, "But the ship's bottom is worn through."

When, in spite of all these warnings, we remained firm in our purpose, and continued the work of getting the *Ayesha* ready for sea, the sporting side of the situation began to appeal to the Englishmen, and they almost ran their legs off in their eagerness to help us. Could it have been gratitude that impelled them to lend us their aid? It is a question I have never been able to answer to my satisfaction, although, to be sure, several of them *did* express a feeling of relief at the thought that now the fatiguing telegraph service with its many hours of overwork, and its lack of diversion, was a thing of the past. They showed us where the provisions and water were kept, and urgently advised us to take provisions from the one side, where they were new and fresh, rather than from the other, where they were stale. They fetched out cooking utensils, water, barrels of petroleum, old clothes, blankets, and the like, and themselves loaded them on trucks and brought them to us. From every side invitations to dinner poured down upon us; my men were supplied with pipes and tobacco; in short, the Englishmen did all they could to help us out.

Nor were they sparing with advice as to the course we ought to take, and time proved that all they told us of wind and weather, of currents, etc., was in every way trustworthy. As the last of our boats left the shore, the Englishmen gave us three hearty cheers, wished us a safe journey, and expressed their gratitude for the "moderation" which we had shown in the discharge of our duty, wherein all of our men had behaved "generously," they said. Then, cameras in hand, they still swarmed about the *Ayesha*, taking pictures of her.

Meanwhile the lookout on our ship reported that the two battling cruisers had come into sight again. From the top of the *Ayesha's* mast I could at first see only the thick cloud of black smoke that the *Sydney's* smoke stack was belching forth, but soon the masts, smoke stacks and upper deck came in sight. Of the *Emden* I could see only one smoke stack and one mast; the rest of the ship was below the horizon. Both cruisers were steering an easterly course, and both were still firing their guns.

Suddenly, at full speed, the *Sydney* made a dash at the *Emden*. "Now," thought I, "the *Emden's* last gun has been silenced, and the *Sydney* is running at her to deal her her death blow." But then, in the black smoke of the English ship, between the foremast and the nearest smoke stack, a tall column of water shot up, which could only be the result of a serious explosion. We supposed that it was caused by a well-aimed torpedo shot from the *Emden*. The *Sydney*, which was still running at a speed of twenty nautical miles, now made a quick turn to starboard, changed her course entirely, and steamed slowly westward. The *Emden* continued to steer an easterly course. Both ships were still firing at each other, but the distance between them grew greater and greater, until finally they were beyond the reach of each other's guns. The fight was over. In the approaching darkness both vessels were soon lost to sight beyond the horizon. That was the last we saw of them. The conflict, which had begun at about 8:30 in the morning, ended at six o'clock in the evening. The report, published in all the English newspapers, that it was only a "sixty minutes' running fight" is therefore to be classed with the many similarly false reports made by the English.

The oncoming darkness now warned me to make my way as speedily as possible out of the harbour, for the dangers of the coral reefs render it unsafe for navigation after nightfall. In the meantime we had taken aboard water enough for four weeks, and provisions for eight. The sails had been bent on as best they could be. I made a short speech, and with three cheers for the Emperor, first in command, the war flag and pennant fluttered up to the masthead of His Majesty's latest ship, the schooner *Ayesha*. "Slowly the steam launch took us in tow. I climbed to the top of the foremast, as from there I could best discern where lay the reefs and the shoals, for of charts we had none. With the boatswain's whistle I gave the launch orders to steer to starboard or to port, according to the lay of the reefs. The *Emden's* two cutters we carried in tow.

Our departure was much too slow to suit us.

The sun was setting, and in these latitudes, so near the equator, there is no twilight. No sooner has the sun disappeared below the horizon than the blackness of midnight reigns. We had not passed quite through the danger zone of the reefs before it grew so dark that, from my position on the foremast, I could not see ahead sufficiently far to direct our course. In order to be able to see anything at all, I climbed down into the port fore channels close by the water, and gave my orders from there.

Just as we were passing the last reef that might prove dangerous to us, we spent some anxious moments. Suddenly, in spite of the darkness, I could see every pebble, every bit of seaweed on the bottom, an unmistakable evidence that we were in very shallow water. Our lucky star guided us over this shoal also, however, and we did not run aground.

Meanwhile we had set some sail, and had thus lightened the work of the steam launch, which still had us in tow. Before long we were free of the sheltering islands, and the long, heavy swells of the ocean put some motion into our new ship.

When we were far enough out at sea to sail our boat without danger of running into the surf to leeward, I called the steam launch back to the ship, so as to take off the crew. The heavy swell made this manoeuvre no light task. Again and again the little steamboat was dashed against the side of the *Ayesha*, and, although the future of the launch was of little interest to me, this unexpected encounter between my old ship and my new one gave me serious concern. I had no confidence in the *Ayesha's* ability to endure with safety such vigorous demonstrations of friendship. Finally, however, we succeeded in ridding ourselves of the steam launch in this way: the last man aboard her started her engine again with the little steam that was left in the boiler. Then, from aboard the *Ayesha*, we reached over with a boat hook, and turned the rudder of the steam launch to port. Curtseying elegantly, the little boat drew away from us, and soon vanished in the darkness. Whither it went, I do not know. In all likelihood it found a grave in the surf that beat wildly only a few hundred metres away. Perhaps, however, it is still beating about the ocean, raiding on its own account.

Chapter 3

On Board

On the following day we undertook a closer inspection of our new abiding place. The *Ayesha* was a ship of 97 tonnage, as we learned from an inscription on one of the beams in the hold. Her length was about thirty metres, and her width somewhere between seven or eight. She was rigged with three masts. Of these, the after two, the mainmast and the mizzenmast, carried only fore and aft sails, whereas the foremast had two square sails. The ship was originally intended to be manned by a crew of five, besides the captain. There were now fifty of us aboard her. Provision for berthing the crew had been made in a special crew's cabin in the extreme forward part of the ship. But here there was room for only six men at the most; the rest of my crew had to sleep in the hold.

When we took possession of the *Ayesha* there was no cargo aboard her—nothing but iron ballast in the hold. Luxurious couches my men surely did not have, for we had brought with us from Keeling but few blankets and mattresses. For the time being, the men slept in a spare sail spread over the iron ballast. In time, however, they would be able to better their condition considerably. They therefore went busily to work at making hammocks out of old ropes which they untwisted, out of twine, and out of old sail cloth torn into strips, and other like material. These hammocks were swung wherever a place could be found for them and afforded the occupants relief from the rather violent motion of the ship.

Below deck, aft of the hold, were two small cabins originally fitted out for sleeping rooms, but in which we were compelled to store our provisions. Moreover, swarms of huge cockroaches made them impossible as living rooms. In the extreme after part of the ship was another small cabin, designated by a sign over the door as navigation room. In it the petty officers were quartered.

On deck was a little deck house. This was divided into two cabins, with a bed in each. One of them I occupied myself; the other was shared by my two lieutenants. Adjoining these cabins was another tiny one, furnished with a table and a few small benches. This served us as mess, as navigation, smoking and wine room, as saloon and for occupation by the officer whose watch it happened to be.

Our commissary department was carried on under many difficulties. To be sure, the canned provisions that we had taken with us from Keeling were of an excellent quality, but the caboose, that is, the ship's kitchen, was, of course, planned for cooking to be done for only five men, and the Lilliputian hearth was in no way sufficient for our needs. Nor could the fresh water we had with us be used for cooking, as the supply was sufficient only for drinking purposes. To enlarge our cooking facilities we brought pieces of iron ballast from the hold, and with this and some strips of tin torn from places in the ship where it was not absolutely necessary, we fashioned a fireproof hearth, and in this improvised fireplace we kindled an open fire. Around it, in a circle, sat the men holding the cooking pots on rods over the fire, until the food was cooked. To set the cooking utensils on the fire and leave them there was quite impossible, as the rolling motion of the ship would soon have dislodged them.

All our cooking was done with salt water. What each day's bill of fare was to be, we left to the decision of the cook. We did not fare poorly on the *Ayesha* by any means. For the most part our meals consisted of rice cooked with fruit, smoked sausage, corned beef, or the like.

The drinking problem was a more difficult one. Aboard our little ship we had found four small iron water tanks in which a supply of fresh water sufficient for a crew of five could easily be carried. These tanks we had not had time to examine while getting the *Ayesha* ready for sea. We had been obliged to fill them as quickly as possible. Now, with the small crew, only one tank had been used, and after a few days we discovered that the other three had become foul. The water we had put into them was therefore unfit to drink. The supply of bottled Seltzer water which I had put aboard at Keeling, I felt must not be used except in case of extreme emergency, for I had to reckon with the possibility that the *Ayesha* might prove unseaworthy, and that we would have to abandon her, and take to the *Emden's* two cutters, that we had aboard. In that case, the bottled water would be all that we could take with us.

We hoped to be able in a reasonably short time to replenish our water supply by refilling with rain-water the three tanks in which the water had fouled. In this hope we were not disappointed. On the thirteenth of November, only four days after our departure from Keeling, the first of the usual tropical rains set in. Our bad tanks had been cleaned in the meantime, and an old sail got ready to catch the rain. It was stretched horizontally across the main hatch. In the middle of the sail was a hole, and directly under this hole a man was stationed with a petroleum can, the kind in which the Standard Oil Company delivers petroleum, and into which the rain-water ran. When it was full, it was passed from hand to hand along a line of men until it reached the tank into which it was to be emptied.

In addition to this, the cabin roof was arranged to catch rain-water. Along the edges of the roof we fastened strips of moulding, and the water which collected on the roof was conducted through two gutters into petroleum cans hung where they emptied. This rain-water was not only fit to drink, but was rendered quite palatable by the addition of a dash of lime juice, of which we had fortunately found a few bottles among the provisions of the former captain.

As, from this time forth, the tropical downpours set in with pleasing regularity, every morning and every evening, our tanks were soon full. In addition to these, all the available utensils and petroleum cans were filled with water. These rainfalls were very welcome for other reasons also. Since all the fresh water had to be reserved for drinking purposes, our prospects for washing seemed rather dubious. Soap will not dissolve in salt water, and to wash with salt water alone is not cleansing. We therefore utilized these tropical downpours to wash ourselves, and as shower baths, our necessity resulting in the invention of a new sort of bath,—a swinging bath. To prevent the rain-water from running off the deck, we stopped up the drain holes, the so-called scuppers, with old rags. With the rolling motion of the ship, the water which had thus been collected on the deck ran from one side to the other, and so gave us a most excellent opportunity for a bath, while the descending rain answered for a final shower.

Moreover, the *Ayesha* carried two small jolly-boats, the one barely large enough to hold two, the other to hold three men. These boats hung on the davits near the deck house. They also were now used to collect water by closing the drain holes with the plugs provided for that purpose. Although we were disappointed to find that the water contained in them was somewhat salty, and therefore unfit to drink, it nevertheless served us very well for washing purposes.

For the ship's service the crew was divided into two watches, a starboard and a port watch. Most of my men were, of course, wholly unused to life on a sailing vessel, and the handling of the gear was entirely new to them. This was particularly the case with the stokers, who, naturally enough, had never seen service on a sailing vessel. Still, there were among the crew a sufficient number of fishermen and seamen who at some former time had served on sailing vessels, to make it possible for me to handle the ship with safety. Whenever there was a job to be done that required great physical strength, every man aboard was available as so much man power.

At first the gear gave us much trouble. Most of the sails were old and rotten, and tore at the slightest provocation, so that we were constantly at work mending and patching the canvas. The tackle also gave way frequently. We were therefore obliged to exercise the greatest care during a squall, as we never knew just how much the masts could bear.

The condition of the ship itself was not such as to inspire one with any great degree of confidence. The captain's opinion, expressed in the words, "The bottom is worn through," as he left the ship, seemed to be well founded. When we went down into the hold and cautiously scraped away at the planking, we discovered that the wood was red and rotten, so much so, indeed, that we quickly stopped our scratching, as we had no desire to poke the point of our knife into the Indian Ocean.

During the first days out we had a heavy swell astern, and the *Emden's* two cutters performed some wonderful dancing at the ends of the long ropes by which we carried them in tow. In one of its wild gyrations one of the cutters took a notion to catch on to the ship, just under the overhanging stern. Usually such set-to's between a ship and its jolly-boat end to the decided disadvantage of the latter, but in this case the conditions were reversed. With a sharp plunge the nose of the boat buried itself in the rotten wood of the stern, and broke a plank above the water line. I had little desire for a repetition of this performance. We therefore set the ill-mannered cutter adrift, and so had but one left, which, for a while, behaved very well. But this proper behaviour was not of long duration, for, seized by an overweening desire for its fellow, no doubt, the remaining cutter departed one night, and carried with it a large piece of the bulwarks to which it had been fastened. And again the break in the ship showed red and rotten wood.

In those first days, the *Ayesha* also leaked badly. In a short time we had so much water in the ship, that it rose to the height of the iron ballast on which the men slept. When we tried to work the ship's pump, we found that it was out of order. The packing of the pistons was gone. So we took the pump to pieces, got the piston out, replaced the missing rubber packing with rags soaked in oil, and finally succeeded in pumping the ship dry. Taking it all in all, the *Ayesha* cut a pretty sorry figure as a ship.

Had we had visitors at this period of our sea voyage, they would have been amazed at the resemblance our costumes bore to those in vogue in the Garden of Eden, for even aside from the times when we took our tropical shower baths—then we wore nothing at all—our clothing was very scant. For the landing at Keeling we had not only clothed ourselves as lightly as possible, but I had given the men orders to wear their oldest clothing. Now, with the continuous handling of the sails, and the other strenuous work aboard the ship, our wearing apparel was fast disappearing. Having neither needles nor thread, we could not even mend it. To be sure, we had some garments that had been given us at Keeling, but these served rather as a source of amusement than as clothing. I had always had the impression that Englishmen generally are tall and spare. Whether those at Keeling were an exception, or what the reason was, I cannot say, but certain it is that most of their trousers reached only to a little below the knees of my men, and their jackets and blouses were big enough for two.

Chapter 4

A Fine Day on Board

Our men rose with the sun, at six o'clock in the morning. On war vessels it is the custom to rouse the crew by a call of three long trills given by all the petty officers at the same time on boatswains' whistles. At this signal the men turn out and lash their hammocks. We gave up the attempt to conform to this custom, as the noise that our one boatswain's whistle could make would hardly have been loud enough to attract the attention of waking men. The crew slept side by side, packed like herrings in a box, and all that was needed to waken the men, was to rouse the first one, who, in rising, could not fail to waken his nearest neighbour, who, in turn, would waken the next, and so on, until the last one was up.

After we were up, the next thing to be done was to wash, provided there was water enough left in the jolly-boats from the night before. If it so happened that we could not get a wash, we accepted the situation with a cheerful spirit, as being quite in harmony with the total absence of toothbrushes aboard the ship. But our hair demanded special attention, for it was growing longer and longer with every day. The only comb that we possessed was passed from hand to hand, each man's neighbour serving him as looking glass, while for hair tonic we had most excellent salt water. There was even a shaving apparatus for the dandies, the rusty condition of the razor, however, making it necessary to use considerable caution.

Then came the cleaning of the ship. Water was hauled up in pails from over the sides of the vessel, and dashed over the deck. A part of the crew set to work at the pumps to rid the ship of the water that had leaked in overnight. The sailors were up in the shrouds, looking after the latest damage that had been sustained there, and making repairs. The cook, in the company of his own chosen helpers, was forward by the caboose, busy with getting breakfast, for which, besides rice, we also had coffee and tea. When this was over, there was really nothing more for the men to do. No drilling could be attempted, for lack of room. So we filled in the time occasionally by initiating the stokers, and others unused to life on a sailing vessel, into the mysteries of steering, of the compass, and of service in the rigging. At other times the one chart of which the ship could boast was fetched out, and the men were shown just where the ship lay. Many an idle hour was spent in making plans for our future.

As for charts, besides special maps of Batavia, where we had no intention of going, there was only the one large map that has been mentioned, which represented the half of the globe, and accordingly was on a very small scale. It began with Hong Kong and Borneo on the east, and ended with Suez, Zanzibar, and Mozambique on the west. The long distance, about 700 nautical miles, to Padang, the port to which I intended to go, was represented on the chart by a space of no more than a hand's breadth.

Meanwhile the dinner hour had arrived. As there were not enough plates, forks, etc., to go round, we ate in relays. Each man's portion was dished out by the cook under supervision of one of the petty officers of the commissary department. With the dinner, a cup of coffee or tea was also served. To while away the long afternoon, we prolonged the meal as much as possible, and, when it was over, usually indulged in an afternoon nap. The separation of officers and crew, as is customary on board ship, was, of course, out of the question with us. The deck space was but just large enough to accommodate all the men with some degree of comfort on the upper deck.

Soon little groups had formed among the men, the members of which gathered each afternoon at some favourite spot. There they would sit or lounge, smoking or sleeping, or happy if it was their turn to have the use of one of the few packs of cards that we had been able to secure before we left Keeling. Some of our men were devoted fishermen. Over the bulwarks, at every available spot, hung the fish lines in waiting for an unwary fish, but I cannot remember that I ever heard of one being caught. Can it be possible that this is to be ascribed to a dislike for rice on the part of the fish? For rice was our only bait. Reminiscences were exchanged, and rebuses, arithmetic questions, conundrums, and the like, went the rounds.

In the evening, after supper was over and the sun was setting, the men usually assembled forward on the deck, and sang. As there were a number of good voices among them, their singing in chorus was very pleasing, and, as usual when Germans are having a good time, the "*Loreley*" and other like tragic songs were those that were oftenest sung. But "*Puppchen*" and the "*Song of the Reeperbahn*" were not neglected.

No particular hour was set for turning in. Everyone lay down to sleep when it suited him best, and the watches, that is, the forward lookout, and the man at the wheel, themselves saw to it that they were relieved at the right time. We carried no lights at night. We had but little petroleum aboard, and the two oil lamps that we had, gave out more smoke than light.

CHAPTER 5

An Uneasy Day

Not always, however, did the days pass as uneventfully as the one just described. Often we had to struggle against high gales and thundergusts. In fact, they had to be reckoned with both morning and evening of every day. As welcome as the thunderstorms were for the supply of fresh water they brought us, we yet looked forward to them with dread also, because of the strain on ship and rigging. In the tropics the coming of a thunderstorm can be seen from afar, and the time of its arrival quite accurately timed.

The approach of one of these storms was usually heralded by a few dark clouds near the horizon, the falling rain showing as a long, broad streak reaching from sky to ocean. As the clouds rose toward the zenith, the columns of rain came visibly nearer. When the storm was within a thousand metres of us, the sails were furled as far as necessary, and we rode out the gale. We "laid to" then, with close reefed sails, the ship's head close to the wind, until the gale, which was always accompanied by a downpour of rain so heavy that we could see nothing except what was immediately in front of us, was over.

One day we had an especially heavy thunderstorm. The clouds hung so low that it seemed as though we could grasp them with our hands. The wind set in more quickly than we had expected, and just as we had begun to shorten our light sails, the tempest was upon us. It seized the mizzen-topsail, and whipped it furiously through the air. The men on deck could not hold it against the strain, it flew over the mizzengaff, caught fast on it, and hung there. To secure it at the time was impossible, because of the heavy rolling of the ship. For a while, the flapping of the sail endangered the whole mizzen-topmast, but more especially the slender upper part of the mast, which is always only lightly stayed. Its violent motion filled us with anxiety. Moreover, we were now in the worst of the gale, and had all we could do to attend to the other sails. Nevertheless, we finally succeeded in furling all the sails with the exception of a few bits of canvas that had to be left out to give the ship steerage way.

The clouds were so heavy that it was almost as dark as night. Unceasingly the lightning flashed about us, followed instantly by a heavy clap of thunder. So near and so vivid werethe flashes of lightning, that they blinded us for the moment, and for seconds at a time we could see nothing at all. It was a genuine little cyclone that was sweeping over us.

Then the violent wind suddenly ceased as the centre of the storm reached us, and the air about us grew absolutely still. The high seas and swells continued, however. The ship, suddenly robbed of its support by the almost instant falling away of the wind, rolled so heavily from side to side, that we feared the masts would go overboard without our being able to do anything to prevent it. The atmosphere was filled with electricity; on each of our mast-heads burned St. Elmo fires, a foot high.

Slowly the thunderstorm passed over. After a few more brief but violent gusts of the recurring gale, the wind died down and blew more steadily and quietly. Soon nothing remained but a few distant flashes of lightning to remind us of the anxious hours we had but just passed. One after the other the sails were set, and we proceeded on our way. But soon afterward, the wind died away entirely.

The times when we were becalmed were perhaps even more unpleasant than when the wind paid us an over-amount of attention, for, with the high and never-ceasing ocean swells, our ship rolled very heavily whenever there was no breeze to drive her. Then the sails, no longer filled by the wind, flapped from side to side, and when the heavy booms went over, the whole ship shivered, and the masts trembled. At such times we often thought it best to furl all sails, and so avoid any possible danger to ship and rigging.

On account of the violent and jerking motion of the ship on such days, life aboard her was extremely unpleasant and very fatiguing. To remain aboard the ship at all, we had to hold on to some support continuously with both hands, or else wedge ourselves firmly into a secure corner.

On this particular day, we were again obliged to furl all sails. While we were thus in the worst of the rolling, and were swearing vigorously at the ship's eccentricities, suddenly a cloud of smoke was reported in sight on the port bow forward. As we were wholly outside of any course ordinarily followed by steamers, we concluded that the vessel sighted must, like ourselves, have reason to avoid the usual routes of steamship travel. At first we thought it might, perhaps, be one of our coaling ships, either the *Exford* or the *Buresk*, which, just before the fight off Keeling, had been dismissed by the *Emden* to await her at certain designated points. Having neither heard nor seen anything of the *Emden*, they might now be running into Padang, hoping there to learn what had happened. On the other hand, it might quite as well be a hostile cruiser that had run into Keeling after the fight, and, having heard of our departure, was now looking for us.

There were, in fact, but three courses for us to choose from while making our escape from Keeling,—to run to Padang, to Batavia, or to Africa. Of these the most probable ones were to Batavia, or to Padang. For a fast cruiser it would be an easy matter to search for us on both of these routes, and so make sure of finding us. Knowing that we were wholly dependent upon the wind for our progress, our pursuers could easily picture to themselves the course we had taken, and where they would most likely find us.

Naturally, we made every effort to discover the character of the unknown vessel. But even from the mast-heads we could see no more than the smoke she was leaving behind her. To elude her by changing our course was quite out of the question with the *Ayesha*, becalmed as we were, and drifting idly. But, after giving us a few anxious hours, the smoke on the horizon vanished.

Meanwhile, the regular evening breeze had set in, and with it came the usual torrents of rain. We were now in the region where the Southeast and Northwest Monsoons meet and struggle for the mastery. The wind changed every few moments. First, a gust would strike the ship from forward, and the next minute it would be blowing a gale from aft, a condition of affairs that afforded opportunity for some expert and ingenious sailing manoeuvres. After we had practised close hauling the sails a number of times, we were suddenly confronted with a task that well nigh proved too much for us. A violent gust of wind from the northwest was sweeping down upon the ship from forward at the same time that one from the south was approaching from aft.

We were therefore obliged to tack by close hauling the foresail, while, at the same time, the mainsail had to be set for wind from astern. The two shower baths that the two gusts brought us could not have been better managed in an up-to-date sanatorium, where alternating hot and cold showers are a feature of the baths. The gust from the northwest brought a torrent of rain so icy cold that most of us got below decks as fast as we could, whereas the one from the south, which overtook us a few minutes later, showered us with water that was more than lukewarm.

Chapter 6

Padang

On the twenty-third of November, early in the morning, the ship was "cleared for action," for we were now getting near land, and it was not at all improbable that we would run across an English or Japanese torpedo boat destroyer coaling somewhere among the islands. For such an emergency my plans were made. I intended to tack ahead of the destroyer, which would certainly not be expecting an attack from us, to bring up alongside of it by an apparently unsuccessful manoeuvre, and then to grapple with the enemy at close quarters. To make the best use of our armament we had cut four holes in the bulwarks of the *Ayesha* where the machine guns could be placed to some advantage, although the rigging, with its lanyards and dead ends, would certainly be a great hindrance. The rifles and pistols were taken up on deck, and the ammunition was set within easy reach. As the machine guns had not been used for some time, a shot was fired from each of them, to test them.

At ten o'clock in the morning the lookout at the mast-head reported: "Land in sight ahead." just where we were, and what land we were approaching, it was quite impossible for us to know, with the limited means of navigation at our command. But to be near any land whatever was a source of satisfaction to us. Gradually, one island after another came in sight. By four o'clock in the afternoon we had got our bearings sufficiently to know that we were just outside of Seaflower Channel, and about eighty nautical miles from Padang.

Of Seaflower Channel we had no charts whatever; we only knew that it abounded in reefs. As a calm always set in towards evening, and I dared not venture to pass at night through this channel so unfamiliar to me, we lay to, and slowly drifted seaward under reefed sails. just before sunrise we turned about, and steered for the Channel again.

Lookouts were stationed in the masts to watch the water for the change in colour that indicates the presence of reefs or shoals. With all sails set, and with a light wind in our favour, we passed through the Channel during the course of the day without meeting with any serious difficulties in the way of navigation.

As we no longer had any reason to fear a shortage in our fresh water supply before reaching Padang, the bottles of Seltzer water were brought out, and one was given to each man, as an especial treat, and probably afforded us more enjoyment than had a bottle of champagne under ordinary circumstances. On that evening, just before seven o'clock, our log registered the eight-hundredth mile.

Before the night was over, a final gale, with a rain like a veritable cloudburst, gave us considerable to do. As the day dawned, the high mountains of Sumatra came in sight against the horizon. Unfortunately, the wind was not only very light, but off shore also, and we could make but little headway. The heat was so intense that towards noon a sail had to be spread for an awning.

Our supply of tobacco had given out entirely by this time. The men smoked tea leaves as a substitute. The officers tried it also, but bah, the devil was welcome to it! The crew seemed to get considerable enjoyment out of it, however.

As a guide for the run into Padang, between all the many reefs and islands, we had drawn a chart for ourselves according to information gathered from an antiquated sailors' hand-book that someone had raked up. Although this chart could lay no claim to being either accurate or complete, it was nevertheless better than none. During the evening we saw, on one of the islands that we passed, a beacon which was wholly a surprise to us. Before the night was over the long-looked-for flash-light of Padang came in sight, but we passed it at a great distance. Much to our regret, the current, instead of taking us toward land, was steadily carrying us farther out to sea, and, with the light breeze that was blowing, to tack was out of the question. By morning, therefore, we were five nautical miles farther off shore than we had been on the previous evening.

The strait in which we now were is the highway for all ships. We had little desire to remain here, if for no other reason than that we were very likely to encounter some hostile cruiser. By this time a complete calm had set in. We therefore lowered our two jolly-boats, the smaller one manned by one, the larger boat by two men, hitched them to our *Ayesha*, and so attempted to make some headway. For the men at the oars, this was no light task, exposed as they were to the full rays of a tropical sun, as they sat unprotected from it in the open boats. We, on board, were not idle either. The oars of the *Emden's* two cutters, which we had with us, were fetched out and tied together by pairs, so as to lengthen them, and with these we proceeded to row the *Ayesha*. Although it cannot be said that we attained the speed of a fast mail steamer in this way, we did, however, make some progress.

On the following day a light wind did at last set in, and relieved us of this strenuous labour. In the distance, near the coast, we saw a number of steamers that were evidently either entering or leaving the port of Padang. One of these roused our interest more than any of the others, because she apparently did not change her position at all, and so was evidently laying to, as the great depth of water in this vicinity precludes the possibility of anchoring. As we drew near to the vessel, we could make out with some degree of certainty that she was not a merchantman. She appeared to be a small warship of some kind—a gun-boat, or a torpedo-boat destroyer, and flew a flag which we could not distinguish, because of its great distance from us.

Suddenly, the ship that had been lying so motionless began to move. Thick clouds of smoke poured from the smokestacks; she turned sharply, headed for us, and approached at high speed. In a short time we recognised the war flag of the Netherlands flying at the masthead. As we had no desire to drop our incognito as yet, and as we were sailing in free waters, there was no reason why we should show our colours. We therefore quickly gathered up all our rifles, and, together with our artillery equipment, stowed them away below decks. All the men quickly disappeared down the main hatchway, which was closed after them. The wildest looking one of the sailors and myself were the only ones who remained in sight. That we both belonged to the Imperial Navy no one would ever have imagined, as our clothing was so scant that we would much more readily have been sized up as belonging to the war fleet of some one of the island kingdoms of the Pacific.

Before long, the torpedo-boat destroyer was close beside us, and began to evince an interest in us, which, inexplicable from the first, soon became extremely embarrassing. At a distance of fifty metres she slowly passed by. On the commander's bridge stood all the officers, each provided with marine glasses, through which they examined our ship with great curiosity. From the lively conversation that was going on between the officers, we concluded that they were talking about us. The destroyer passed around us, close under our stern, and all the binoculars were turned toward our ship's name, which had long since disappeared under a coat of the thickest white paint. We were just congratulating ourselves that we had bluffed her, when, at a distance Of 5,000 metres, she suddenly turned, and lay to. At this, I could not rid myself of the thought that we had been expected.

At the destroyer's approach we had got our war flag ready to run up, for if we had been spoken, we would, of course, have replied by a display of our colours.

In the course of the afternoon our attendant, whom by this time we had identified by the ship's name as the Dutch destroyer, *Lynx*, left us, and disappeared in the direction of Padang. In our cheerful but overhasty conclusion that she was preceding us into port to give notice of our coming, so that maids of honour might be in waiting, and triumphal arches be prepared for us, we were doomed to disappointment, however.

By nightfall we lay close before the small, flat coral islands that lie in front of the entrance to the harbour. We could see the lights of a steamer that was coming out of the harbour. Another was moving into port. We looked upon both of them with suspicion, as we supposed one of them to be our companion of the foregoing afternoon. We therefore carefully screened the *Ayesha's* lights. We had made no mistake, for in signalling to the incoming steamer, the outgoing ship revealed herself to be our old acquaintance, the *Lynx*. To our regret, she had sighted us in spite of all the precaution we had taken. Again she became our close companion, and for a while her green and red side lights could be seen immediately astern, at a distance of not more than one hundred metres. We felt truly sorry for the *Lynx*. It must have been very irritating to her to have to trundle behind us at the wonderful speed of one nautical mile, a speed which, with the light breeze blowing, the *Ayesha* could not exceed. The engineers at the 1,000 horse-power engines of the *Lynx* probably wished us elsewhere more than once that night.

In so far as our problems of navigation were concerned, the presence of the *Lynx* was a distinct advantage to us, for we were sailing in waters with which we were wholly unacquainted, but we could feel perfectly sure that wherever the *Lynx* could float, we could also. We knew that if we were nearing a shoal, our escort would retreat in time, and we could then turn and follow her.

Otherwise, however, her companionship was little to our liking, for it gave us the appearance of a disreputable little vagabond being brought in by a burly policeman. As we were a warship, we had no intention of allowing ourselves to be thus escorted. I therefore determined to communicate with the *Lynx* by signal. For this purpose I had a white bull's eye lantern, that usually hung in the men's quarters, brought on deck. In front of this lantern we held a board, and by raising and lowering it, we gave our Morse signals. By means of this apparatus of high technical development, we conveyed to our escort the message in English, "Why are you following me?"

Although the *Lynx* acknowledged our signal as having understood it, we received no reply to our question. After a half hour had passed without an answer, we resorted to our Morse signal again, but this time asked in German, "Why do you follow me?" And again the signal was acknowledged, but no answer given. Shortly afterward, however, the *Lynx* increased her speed, and steamed off. For another whole day the poor *Lynx* had to dog our footsteps, for the wind continued to fail us.

When, on the following day, the *Ayesha* had carried us within the limits of Dutch territorial waters, we immediately ran up our war flag and pennants. The *Lynx* did not again draw near to us, but kept at a distance of several thousand metres.

Toward noon we found ourselves in a position of some peril. We were aware that we were now in a region of submerged reefs over which a vessel of even our light draught could not pass in safety, but of the exact location of these reefs we knew nothing. To our great relief, a little Malay sailboat came alongside, and brought us a native pilot, whom I was glad to employ. The only prospect of remuneration that I could hold out to him was through our consul, as the entire amount of cash on board consisted of a shilling and twopence, which we had found in a pocket-book that the former captain had forgotten to take with him, and which we had confiscated for the benefit of the Imperial treasury. In marked contrast to the impression we made on the Dutch—as developed later—this Malay pilot, who seemed to us to be a very intelligent person, was from the outset untroubled by any doubt of our status as a German warship, for he at once declared himself willing to accept our promise of a later payment through the German consul.

Hardly had the pilot come alongside, when the *Lynx* made a dash for us at high speed. As we had no idea what her intentions were, I ordered the war flag, which had been lowered in the meantime, to be run up again. In order to impress the *Lynx* more fully with the fact that she was dealing with an Imperial ship of war, I ordered the salute customary between warships to be given, as she sped past us at a distance of about sixty metres. Our entire crew stood at attention on deck, and our officers saluted. The *Lynx* at once returned our salute in like manner.

Just before running into the harbour, I flagged a signal to the *Lynx*, saying, "I am sending a boat." Then I donned my full-dress uniform—my khaki brown landing suit from the *Emden*, of which I had been most careful and went on board the *Lynx*.

Her commander received me at the gangway ladder, and escorted me to, the messroom. I opened the conversation, saying that we had felt much flattered at the lively interest he had shown in us during the past day and a half, that we were a landing squad from the *Emden*, and were on the way to Padang with His Majesty's ship, *Ayesha*, that at Padang we wished to repair damages, and relieve the distress on board by replenishing our store of provisions and our water supply. I then inquired whether he knew of any reason why we could not run into the harbour. To this the commander replied that he had orders to accompany us, that there was nothing to prevent us from running into the harbour, but that in all probability we would not be allowed to run out again; that these matters would, however, be decided by the civil authorities on shore, and that he could give us neither further, nor more definite, information.

I represented to him that the *Ayesha*, being a warship, could leave the harbour at any time, and that no one had the right to detain us. Then I added in jest: "I hope you and I will not get into a fight when I run out."

As I left the destroyer, I saw the *Ayesha* for the first time from a distance, and under full sail. I must say that she made a capital appearance, and looked very pretty, even though the patched and torn sails she carried were little in harmony with the pennant and war flag of the German Empire.

Just before we reached the entrance to the harbour, a small steam tug came out to meet us. It was bringing the harbour master, who was coming to show us where to drop anchor. He indicated a place quite far out. It was my intention, however, to get as close as possible to the steamships lying in the harbour, for even now I could distinguish the German and Austrian flags flying on some of them. I therefore told the harbour master that I would rather not anchor so far out, but would like to run farther into the harbour. It was not a sufficiently sheltered place for my ship, I explained, and furthermore, that it required a great length of chain to anchor in water of that depth. That our chains were in fact quite long enough to reach to the bottom of water six times as deep, I did not feel obliged to tell him.

By and by his objections were overcome by argument in plain German. But, as we got farther in, he demanded very insistently that we anchor at once. Now it chanced that by a mishap the two topsails, the very ones by which a ship makes the most headway, absolutely refused to come down. Again and again the sheets and halyards hitched, so that, as was my original intention, we had come close up to the steamers before we found it possible to anchor.

As soon as the *Ayesha* lay at anchor, I sent my senior officer, Lieutenant Schmidt, on shore to report our arrival officially, and to make my wishes known to the authorities. At the same time, the German consul was asked to come on board. Furthermore, I announced that, in accordance with international custom) no one would be allowed to come on board without the permission of the government authorities, nor would anyone from the ship be permitted to go ashore.

Soon the *Ayesha* was surrounded by boats coming from the German ships. There were the *Kleist*, the *Rheinland*, and the *Choising* of the Lloyd line, besides an Austrian ship. They all had their top flags set, and greeted us with a "Hurrah." Cigars; cigarettes, tobacco, watches, clothing, poems, letters, and, what we wanted most of all, German newspapers, were thrown to us. That these were old, none later than the second of October, and it was now the twenty-seventh of November, mattered little. They were most welcome, for up to this time, the only news that we had obtained was from the English papers that we had found on board the English steamers that the *Emden* had raided.

All that we had heard of the war, therefore, were the widely disseminated Reuter tales of horror such as: The Russians near Berlin—the *Kaiser* wounded—the Crown Prince fallen—suicide epidemic among German generals—revolution in Germany—the last horse slaughtered—complete rout on the western front, and the like. Together with the newspapers, many pictures had been thrown on board also, and, on coming into the cabin and mess soon afterward, I found the walls covered with pictures of the *Kaiser*, the chief of the fleet, the Secretary of State for the Imperial Navy, and others, which the men had tacked up for decoration.

At first the Dutch Government authorities made trouble for us, as they were not disposed to accord us the status of a warship, but intended to regard us as a prize of war. Against this, I made an instant and vigorous protest by declaring that it was only to my superior officers in Germany that I would have to account for my right to command this ship.

At the same time I asked permission to take aboard water, provisions, ropes, sailcloth, clothing, nautical charts, and the simplest toilet necessities, such as soap, tooth brushes, hair brushes, shoe polish, etc. The German consul took charge of this. The "neutrality officer," especially appointed by the Dutch government to look after such matters, immediately wired to Batavia to get his orders concerning us direct from the authorities there. Altogether, the impression I received was that every effort was being made to hold the *Ayesha*, and to intern the officers and crew. It was very evident that the local authorities were much disturbed, and feared complications with Japan or England, if we were allowed to leave.

The person most concerned, and the one with whom the decision lay, seemed to be the harbour master, a subaltern official, and a Belgian at that. When the afternoon had well nigh passed, and the things ordered for the ship had not arrived, I requested the senior Dutch commander at Padang to order the goods to be delivered at once, as, in conformity to the neutral code, I would have to run out of the harbour within twenty-four hours. Finally, at seven o'clock in the evening, a part of what had been ordered arrived, and with the things came the neutrality officer. He made every possible effort to induce me to allow officers and crew to be interned. As I had foreseen this, my officers had been asked to be present and take part in the conversation, so that he might be convinced from the beginning that the *Ayesha's* officers were unanimous in refusing to consider his proposition.

In the first place, the neutrality officer represented to me—in so far as I could see, by advice from Batavia—how wholly impossible it would be for us to get away, as it was forbidden to deliver either marine charts, or nautical books. There were many other things also with which we could not be supplied, such as clothing, for instance, since, to provide us with these, as well as with soap, tooth powder, etc., would be to "increase our war strength."

As it had now been three weeks since any of us had been able to brush our teeth, we decided that this hardship could be endured a little longer. Nor had the one comb we possessed failed to serve our

Von Mücke

modest demands. As the harbour master had seen that my men were going almost naked for want of clothing, and as he also was aware that we had no marine charts, I could but conclude that there was intention in refusing us these very necessary articles. When I persisted in my determination to sail with or without charts, I was told that we could not escape capture if we ran out, as the waters round about were being scoured by Japanese and English cruisers; that it had only been by a lucky chance that we had escaped capture so far, and that we would surely be caught if we put to sea again; that the *Emden* had acquitted herself well enough, and that no one would criticize us if this hopeless attempt were abandoned. It is needless to say that we absolutely refused to be moved by all this persuasion.

Meanwhile, the provisions had been delivered and stowed away on board, and the ship made ready to weigh anchor, the only hindrance to our departure being the ten live pigs that we had taken with us, for they persisted in standing just where our anchor chain was being hove up. At eight o'clock in the evening we left our anchorage.

From the Dutch papers that we received a few weeks later, we learned that the people had occupied themselves with various speculations as to what we were going to do, and where we were bound. They might have spared themselves the trouble of these speculations if they had listened as we departed, for the answer to the question whither we were going and what were our intentions, was born back to them upon the breeze, as the *Ayesha* vanished into the night:

To the Rhine, the Rhine, the German Rhine,
To guard its sacred boundary line!"

Chapter 7

The Meeting With the "Choising"

With a light wind astern, the Ayesha slowly made her way out from among the Dutch islands, and toward three o'clock in the morning had passed beyond the limits of Dutch territorial waters. I had but just turned in when Lieutenant Schmidt, whose watch it was, waked me with the words: "Captain, a German boat is coming alongside."

As I knew that we were then well out at sea, I growled out: "Man, don't talk nonsense! Let me sleep!"

But he assured me again that it was as he had said, and would not be frightened off even by the most violent protests. At the same time I heard loud voices from outside crying: "There she is, there she is! We have caught her after all."

As I came on deck, I saw a little rowboat with a few people in it swiftly approaching us from out the darkness of the lingering night. Soon one travelling case, and then another, came flying on board. Their two owners appeared immediately afterward, and turned out to be an officer of the reserves and a chief engineer's mate, also a reservist. Both reported to me for duty. As we were outside of the limit of Dutch territorial waters, there was no reason for deferring their enrolment.

Our only difficulty was to provide quarters for the officers now aboard the *Ayesha*, as there was but the one bed, which was hardly big enough for three. In the end, it was arranged that one officer should sleep in the bunk in the cabin, while another chose the place on the floor under the mess table for his bed, a resting place which was not wholly free from disturbance, however, as the third officer, who had the watch, was inclined to put his feet there.

By evening, a moderate, favourable breeze had taken us as far as Seaflower Channel, with which we were well acquainted. To our surprise, we discovered a large steamer coming toward us on an easterly course. As there are no beacon lights on this strait, it is avoided by steamers, most merchantmen preferring to go by way of the more northerly route through Siberut Strait, where there are many lights. The appearance of a steamer in this unfrequented spot was, therefore, to say the least, rather remarkable. I strongly suspected it to be a warship.

As quickly as possible every sail, to the very last rag we had, was set, our course was changed hard to starboard, and, with all the speed we could muster, we tried to get back into Dutch waters. To our great relief, the low, palm-covered coral islands soon came into sight, easily distinguishable by the broad white line of the surf that always breaks on their shores. We crept as close as we dared to this line of surf, keeping at a distance of about a thousand metres from the shore. To anchor in this depth of water was quite impossible, for these coral islands rise abruptly, almost perpendicularly, out of the water.

Our frame of mind was in no wise improved when suddenly our unknown steamer began to exchange flashlight signals in secret code with some other vessel as yet invisible to us. Soon afterward the second warship, for it could be no other kind of vessel, steamed away toward the south, while the other cruised back and forth through Seaflower Channel. Unfortunately the wind died down more and more, so much so that our hope that by daylight we would be out of sight of the cruising steamer, was doomed to disappointment.

It was my intention now to run in between the many small islands, to tie the *Ayesha* fast to the first convenient palm tree, take down topmasts and sails, and so make it impossible to discover us from out at sea. Then I meant to find out the nature of the ship in which we were so much interested. The calm which set in rendered it impossible to carry out this plan, however. At sunrise we were only a few nautical miles distant from the warship, and hardly had the daylight revealed to her the masts of the *Ayesha*, when she changed her course and approached us at high speed. We were still within the limit of Dutch territorial waters, and I had not the least desire to leave them. Fortunately for us, the man-of-war turned out to be neither English nor Japanese. It was the Dutch flag-ship, *De Zeven Provincien*. The iron-clad followed us, always at some distance, however, until we had left Dutch waters in our course westward.

We continued to sail toward the west, intending to keep the *Ayesha* within the vicinity of a certain point where we hoped to meet with some German steamer. Although it had not been possible for us to make any definite arrangements with any of the German vessels that were lying at Padang, nevertheless, from the conversations that had taken place from deck to deck, their captains had some knowledge of the course we intended to follow. We took it for granted, therefore, that some one of these steamers would follow us with a view of aiding us on our farther journey. So we drifted about at sea for nearly three weeks. During a part of this time we had rough weather, which was especially trying to our ten pigs, for whom quarters had been put up in the bows near the capstan. To make life aboard the *Ayesha*, when she was rolling heavily, at all endurable to these animals, we had nailed slats on the flooring of their quarters. Before this had been done, the poor creatures went sliding back and forth across the smooth deck, from rail to rail.

Twice our hope that a friendly steamer was coming to our relief was disappointed. Each time it was an English ship. One of them behaved so peculiarly, and made such unusual manoeuvres as we came in sight, that we believed her to be an auxiliary cruiser. We therefore cleared the *Ayesha's* deck for action. To occupy the attention of the cruiser, with whom we wished to pass for a harmless merchant vessel, we signalled: "Please give me the geographical position." This is a signal very commonly used by sailing vessels when meeting a steamer. The desired information was given us, but with it came the embarrassing question: "Who are you?" We had no special signal of our own, and the *Ayesha's* signal, which we had learned from the ship's papers, we did not, for obvious reasons, care to give.

So we took four flags that happened to be at hand, arranged them one above the other, tied a knot in the two upper ones, so that no one could tell what they were, and then hoisted this signal in such a way that it was half hidden by the sails. This scheme we hoped would lead the steamer to believe that we had answered the question, but that she had failed to decipher our signal. About half an hour later the steamer had disappeared. We saw her answering signal, "I have seen your signal, but cannot make it out," fluttering after her at half mast as long as she remained in sight. The second English steamer came in view at a great distance from us, and probably did not see us at all.

The fourteenth of December, 1914, was a thick, foggy and rainy day, with rather high seas running. The *Ayesha* was tacking back and forth under close reefed sails, when suddenly, through the dense atmosphere, we could see, only about four thousand metres ahead, a steamer looming up out of a thick, gray fog bank. She had two masts and one smoke stack, and was steering an easterly course. We were sailing toward the west. At this point the course of the ordinary merchantman can only be either to the north, or to the south. Hence, a steamer running on an easterly course here, must have some unusual reason for doing so. The natural inference was that this was one of the German steamers looking for us. We steered our course for her at once, under as much sail as our ship could carry. We sent off red and white fire balls that are visible by day as well as by night, in the hope of attracting the attention of the steamer, which by this time we had recognized as the Lloyd steamer, *Choising*. Our great fear was that the *Choising* would fail to see us in the foggy weather, and so would pass us by. At last, after we had sent off our fourth or fifth fire ball signal, we saw the ship turn, and come towards us.

Up flew our flag and pennant. The steamer ran up the German flag. The crew laid aloft into the shrouds, and three cheers rang from deck to deck. As usual, our men were dressed in the manner customary in the Garden of Eden, a costume which necessity had forced upon them. The men of the *Choising* confided to us later that they were blank with astonishment when suddenly, out of the fog, emerged a schooner, the shrouds of which were filled with naked forms. Because of the heavy seas running, an immediate transfer to the *Choising* was not possible. As better weather had prevailed in the region to the south, from which we had come, I signalled the *Choising* to follow the *Ayesha.*

But, instead of growing better, the weather grew steadily worse on the following day, until, during the course of the night, it developed into a heavy storm. The *Ayesha's* sails were close reefed, and, it must be said, she behaved well. Not one of the heavy combers broke over her; she rode them like a duck. Of course, the inside of the ship was as wet as the outside, for the spray dashed over the deck without intermission.

At daybreak the *Choising*, which is a ship of 1,700 tonnage, signalled by flag: "On account of the storm and heavy seas I cannot remain here." I therefore decided to run in under the lee of the land, so as to make the transfer there, and accordingly, signalled another place of meeting to the *Choising*. The two ships separated again, as I, in my sailing vessel, could not steer the same course that the steamer took.

The next night was the worst that we experienced on the *Ayesha.* All night long the tempest raged. Although aware of our proximity to the islands, we did not know just where we were. Both the wind and the current threatened to dash us against the reefs. The night was so black that we could not see anything. If, under these conditions, we should get too near the shore, both ship and crew were doomed. Even the small rags of sails, closely reefed as they were, which we still carried, were almost too much. Towards morning an especially fierce squall set in. It was too much for our rotten old sails. We heard a sharp crack, and then another,—our foresail and our staysail had torn away from their bolt ropes, and only a few small rags were left whipping in the wind. The departing foresail took with it a third sail, the fore staysail, so that we lost all our forward canvas. To set a spare sail was quite impossible at the time, both on account of the darkness and of the heavy running seas. We had to lay to, therefore, with only the aftersails, and trust to luck to keep away from the surf.

As soon as the day dawned, the spare sails were got out and bent on. Before long, the wind began to die down. We found it possible to increase our canvas and steer toward the place appointed for our meeting with the *Choising*. As we drew near to it, at about nine o'clock in the morning, the *Choising* appeared in the distance. In the meantime, however, the wind had fallen off so completely that the *Ayesha* could hardly make any headway at all. I therefore signalled the *Choising* to take us in tow, and get in the lee of the nearest island. There we would find shelter from both wind and waves, and the transfer could be safely made.

Chapter 8

The Passing of the "Ayesha"

While we were being towed by the *Choising*, we began to unrig the good old *Ayesha*. It saddened us to think that we would have to sink her, as there was no port to which we could take her. There was danger that she would be restored to her former owner if we took her to a Dutch port. This we wanted to prevent under any circumstances. All the provisions we still had on hand were placed on the upper deck, and our arms were taken there also. Trunks there were none to pack. The *Ayesha's* figure-head, which represented the favourite wife of the prophet, was taken down, and the rudder wheel unscrewed; both were to be carried with us aboard the *Choising*, and kept as souvenirs.

Soon we had reached the shelter of the small islands, the swell ceased, and it was possible to bring the *Ayesha* alongside the steamer. Meanwhile, the *Ayesha's* shrouds, the ropes which hold the masts, were cut, and all other ends and stays were either removed, or cut through. At the same time two holes were bored into the hold, and through these the ship began slowly to fill.

Towards four o'clock in the afternoon the *Choising's* engine was started up, and the *Ayesha* was cut adrift. It appeared as though the little ship were loath to part from us, for, although our steamer was moving on, and no hawser was holding the *Ayesha* to us, she kept alongside the *Choising* for some time. And then, at last, as though she had found her own strength insufficient to keep up with us, the *Ayesha* caught on to our ship, just behind the gangway ladder, carrying a part of it with her.

I wanted to stay by the *Ayesha* as long as she was afloat, so our steamer was stopped, and we lay to at a distance of three hundred to four hundred metres off from her. The loss of the brave little ship touched us deeply. Although our life on board had been anything but comfortable, we nevertheless all realized fully that it was to the *Ayesha* we owed our liberty. For nearly a month and a half she had been our home. In that time she had carried us 1709 nautical miles. We all stood aft at the stern railing of the *Choising*, and watched the *Ayesha's* last battle with the waves. Gradually, and very slowly, she sank lower and lower in the water. Soon it washed her upper deck. Then suddenly a shudder passed over the whole ship; she seemed to draw a long breath; the bow rose out of the water for a last time, only to plunge into it again the more deeply. The iron ballast rolled forward; standing on end, her rudder up, her masts flat on the water, the *Ayesha* shot like a stone into the deep, never to be seen again. Three cheers for her rang out above her ocean grave.

The day was the sixteenth of December, 1914, and the hour, fifty-eight minutes after four o'clock in the afternoon.

Aboard the *Choising*, the first thing to be done was to order a course to the west, and the next, to see what provision could be made for my men. A place had already been prepared for them in a part of the ship ordinarily used for the storing of coal. It had been cleaned up, and mattresses, blankets, etc., sufficient for all, were in readiness, so that, in comparison with the days spent on the *Ayesha*, a life of luxury was before us.

An ocean greyhound my new ship surely was not. When in the best of trim, she went at the rate of seven and one half miles, but there were times when we had to content ourselves with four. This was due, in part, to poor coal. The *Choising* was a ship that had originally been intended for use as a coaling steamer for the *Emden*, and in this capacity had waited long for her at the appointed place. But, as the British Admiralty had been so obliging as to provide the *Emden* most generously and considerately with the best of Welsh coal, although its intended destination was Hong Kong, there had been no reason why the *Emden* should take on any of the poor quality of coal from India and Australia, which the *Choising* had aboard for her. While waiting for the *Emden* the *Choising's* cargo of coal had got on fire, and we were now using what was left of this half-burned coal.

On the *Choising* we had news which was of importance to us. At the time that we left Padang in the *Ayesha*, we found it a most difficult problem to decide where to go. My earliest plan, to try to reach Tsing-tao, had to be abandoned when, at Padang, we learned of the fall of that colony. My next intention was to join His Majesty's ship *Königsberg*, of whose whereabouts we knew nothing more than that she was somewhere in the Indian Ocean. In case she was no longer there (I had hoped to get news of her from the *Choising*), my next plan was to sail to German East Africa. We knew that there had been some severe fighting there between our colonial troops and the English, and, upon reflection, I abandoned this project also, as being an absolutely hopeless one. With only fifty men, whose clothing outfit was an entirely inadequate one, and who were wholly unprovided with any of the many things necessary to troops on land, with neither surgeon nor medicines, no knowledge of the language, no guide, and no maps, it would be next to impossible, in a district as large as the fighting area of Southeast Africa, to locate and make connection with troops numbering not more than a few thousands themselves.

For the present, therefore, there was but one course left open to us,—to make our way homeward by following the route around Africa. How to provision our ship for so long a journey was a problem which suggested many difficulties, however.

But at last we found in one of the newspapers the report of a battle between Turkish and British troops at Sheikh Said, near Perim, an island in the Strait of Bab-el-Mandeb (Gate of Tears). This gave us reason to believe that Turkey also had now entered the war. Our diligent search for confirmation of this surmise was finally rewarded by finding in one of the papers the announcement that war between the Turkish and British Empires had begun. The new situation thus created suggested a landing in Arabia as our nearest and most hopeful prospect. The course which appeared to be even more reasonable, *viz.*, to join the *Königsberg*, was abandoned, in the first place, because the *Choising* had brought word that the *Königsberg* had been sunk in battle somewhere to the north of Australia, and in the second place, because of news that she was bottled up in the Rufiji River. If she had been sunk, our search for her would be to no purpose, and if she was shut in by a blockade, she would neither have coal, nor could she use any that we might bring her. The fifty men whom we should add to her numbers would only make so many more mouths to feed.

The *Choising* was therefore started on a southerly course, in the first place, to avoid the principal steamer routes, and secondly, to keep out of the region in which the tropical cyclones are most frequent, for the *Choising* was not equal to such a tempest. A sharp lookout was kept, so that we might catch sight of an enemy's ship before we ourselves were discovered. On account of our ship's remarkable speed, the only chance of escape we had, in case we came in contact with a hostile man-of-war, lay in a game of bluff.

The *Choising* was still painted like all Lloyd steamships, *viz.*, black hull, white bulwarks, and ochre brown trimmings. Of course, we could not in safety continue like that. So we gave our ship a coat of paint that made her look like a Dutchman. But on second thought, we concluded that this was hardly safe, as we were likely to meet a number of vessels in the Strait of Bab-el-Mandeb, and that some of them might ask us the question, "Who are you?" which already had proved so embarrassing to us. We had no record of seagoing ships on board, except an English list, at the end of which we found the names of a number of English vessels that had been sold by the English to foreign countries. Among these there was one steamship, the *Shenir*, that had been sold to a Genoa firm, and that was a vessel of 1700 tons. As this was the exact size of the *Choising*, we decided to adopt the *Shenir* as sponsor for our ship, and ere long the legend, *Shenir*, Genoa, in large white letters, adorned our stern.

This discovery we had made in the English shipping list was especially welcome to me, as I preferred to pass for an Italian. In view of Italy's attitude of vacillation, I had reason to believe that even an English warship would hesitate unnecessarily to harass an Italian vessel.

The *Shenir*, from Genoa, would naturally be expected to fly the Italian flag. But this was an article which, unfortunately, was not numbered among the possessions of the *Choising*. Nor was there any green bunting on board. A green window curtain was discovered by someone, however, and to it we sewed a strip of red, and a strip of white bunting. A committee was then selected from among the men who had artistic ability, and they were soon hard at work painting Italy's coat of arms upon the white strip. The green of the curtain was not of the right shade, however, so we added some yellow paint to a pot of blue, which we happened to have on board, until the desired shade of green was produced, and then dipped the green part of the flag into it.

Chapter 9

From Perim to Hodeida

January 7th, 1915, found us in the vicinity of the Straits of Perim. Nothing worthy of note had happened on the way. A number of steamers had been sighted, but always in time to change the course of our vessel toward the coast of Africa. We kept this course until the steamer had disappeared, when we promptly returned to the right one.

Christmas was a very quiet day with us, but our New Year's festivities were all the more hilarious, and we made the most of what little remained of beer and wine aboard the *Choising*.

It had been my intention to arrive in the Perim Straits immediately after sundown. In this we were not quite successful, however, and again for the reason that we had no marine charts. just as once before we had to draw a chart for ourselves when running into Padang, so now we had been obliged to make one of the Red Sea, and, naturally, our knowledge of the *Choising's* position was not quite accurate. As a consequence, we arrived at the Straits of Perim a few hours too early. I therefore gave orders to turn about and cruise back and forth a while. A large steamer coming from Dachibuti gave us some anxious moments, for we took her to be a man-of-war. She turned out to be a French mail steamer, however. As soon as darkness set in, we steered for the Straits of Perim again, and proceeded at high speed.

I had counted with certainty upon meeting with some sort of patrol in the Straits. In that event we would have been quite helpless, for with the *Choising* we could not face even the smallest hostile war vessel. We could not so much as run away, for any steam launch could have overtaken us. As my chief purpose was to conduct my men to where they could again serve in defence of their country, I determined, if necessary, to sacrifice the *Choising*.

In case we should meet a hostile ship close to the African coast, I intended to strand our vessel and leave her there, taking the men with me in the long boats. We should then be ashore in the enemy's territory, and free to do as we might deem best. Should we be overtaken on the northerly side of the Straits, it was my intention to run boldly into the Perim harbour, trusting in Heaven for the outcome, or, if I failed in this, I proposed to run the steamer aground, and venture a bold attack upon the telegraph station which we knew was located in this vicinity. To be prepared for any emergency, the *Choising's* three largest long boats were swung out, lowered to the bulwarks, and made fast. Water, provisions for eight weeks, arms and ammunition, besides a few personal belongings, were stowed away in the boats.

An officer was placed in command of each one of them, and a particular crew designated for duty in it. The only orders given to the boats' crews were, once for all: "Obey your officer."

And again, as darkness came on, we were in much uncertainty with regard to our ship's position. Ahead of us we saw a group of small islands which, we concluded, must be the "Seven Brothers" lying just at the entrance of the Straits. In truth, however, these were the Arabian mountains, whose highest peaks rose into view just above the horizon, a fact which we did not discover until we came in sight of the Perim revolving light. This gave us a good fixed point from which to direct our further course.

Naturally, as we approached the Straits, all hands were on deck. Everyone was keeping a sharp lookout, for our only hope of safety lay in the keenness of our observation. The ship's lights were closely screened. The officers and petty officers were given orders to make continual rounds through the vessel to see to it that not a single ray of light escaped to reveal our presence, for the Chinese crew of the *Choising* had little appreciation of the importance of this precaution.

Whether I should sail with or without lights had been a question to which I had given much careful thought. If I calmly proceeded with all lights showing, just as any ordinary merchantman would, it might chance that none of the English patrol ships would hold me up, as it was not at all likely that so small a merchant ship as the *Choising* would be regarded with suspicion. A ship sailing with screened lights would, on the contrary, become an object of suspicion to anyone who should discover her. Nevertheless, in the end, I decided to have the lights screened.

The Strait of Bab-el-Mandeb is a very narrow water-way. I hugged the African shore as closely as possible, to take advantage of the darker horizon there, and also because the shore afforded a dark background for the ship. But in spite of all this exercise of caution, we got so near to the revolving light at Perim that its intermittent ray fell upon us like a searchlight, illuminating us for seconds at a time. Moreover, we could see two English warships lying just outside of Perim, and they were signalling to each other in Morse code. During that night's most anxious half hour we muttered many a bitter imprecation upon our engine that at best could make no more than seven and a half miles. But fortune favoured us; the Englishmen did not discover us. Perhaps none of the small patrol boats upon which I had reckoned were abroad, for there was a stiff breeze blowing, and the sea was running high. At the end of two trying hours we had got to where we could consider ourselves as safely through.

In the broader expanse of the Red Sea I kept well without the regular steamship course, and on the eighth of January, just after dark, we lay with the *Choising* close to Hodeida. The only book that we had from which to inform ourselves with regard to Arabian ways and customs was a "round the world" guide book that would have answered the purpose of directing a wedding journey very well. From it we learned that Hodeida is a large commercial city, and that the Hejaz railroad to Hodeida was in course of construction. As the book was some years old, and as one of my officers remembered that years ago he had met a French engineer who told him that he had been engaged in the construction of a railroad to Hodeida, we took it for granted that the railroad was completed by this time. Even should we be wrong in, our supposition, we would still, in all likelihood, be able to get some news of the war, and, in case we should have to continue our journey on the *Choising*, we would at least be able to secure charts of the Red Sea.

As we approached Hodeida, or more accurately speaking, as we approached the locality where we expected to find Hodeida—because of our constant lack of marine charts we were never certain of just where we were—we suddenly beheld a long line of electric lights along the shore. Great was our joy at this first sign of a return to civilization. That Hodeida would be provided with electric lights had not entered into our most hopeful expectations.

"It appears to be a very respectable kind of place after all," was the opinion expressed on the bridge. "There even are electric lights. Then surely the railroad will be running. I can see ourselves walking into the central railroad station of Hodeida to-morrow morning, and boarding the special express. In a fortnight we shall be on the North Sea again."

We supposed the row of lights we saw to be on the Hodeida dock, for our "round the world" guide book had told us that Hodeida is a seaport. As we came closer to this dock, my joy gave way to apprehension, for, as I looked, the lights of the dock seemed suddenly and strangely to move closer together, an eccentricity which is not usual with lights on a dock. As we were quite sober, we decided that it must be the dock that was at fault. I therefore gave orders to stop the *Choising*, so that soundings might be taken, from which to learn how far we were from the shore. A depth of forty metres was reported. Now we were evidently only a few thousand metres off from the supposed dock, while, according to the soundings, there must be a distance of several nautical miles between us and the shore. As we realized this, the dock lost much of its attractiveness in our eyes. It must be something else. I gave orders:

"Course, to the south!" and ran off a few nautical miles.

I then ordered the four long boats that had been kept in readiness ever since our approach to Perim, to be lowered, and my men got into them. The captain of the *Choising* received written orders to take his ship farther out to sea, to spend the next two days in the vicinity of a given point outside of the usual steamship course, and on each of the succeeding nights to return to the place where my men and I had left the ship, and await us there. If we did not return, he was to proceed to Massowa. My reason for wishing the *Choising* to return during the next two nights, was our total lack of any definite knowledge as to who was in control in South Arabia. Our latest information in regard to the war was over three months old, and although it had told of battles between the Turks and the English, the outcome of these battles was unknown to us. It was therefore quite possible that Hodeida was now in the hands of the English. In that event, it was my intention to return to the *Choising* on one of the following nights, and to continue our journey aboard her. The days, I meant to spend somewhere in the desert, in hiding.

At the same time, I arranged for signals by rockets to be given the *Choising* in case I should learn of the proximity of hostile ships that might prove dangerous to her. There was one special signal that meant: "Enemy's ships near. Proceed at once to Massowa." I wanted to avoid exposing the ship unnecessarily to the danger of capture while returning for us.

Soon the *Choising* had vanished in the darkness of the night, and my little flotilla of long boats was being vigorously rowed toward the shore. The ship's boats, like all boats that have been out of the water for some time, leaked badly, although days before we left the *Choising* they had been wet both inside and out, had been freshly painted, and kept half filled with water. Our chief effort for the time being was therefore directed toward bailing out the boats. As soon as the day dawned, all sails were set in the boats of our flotilla, and a goodly regatta in the direction of the shore developed.

On our supposed dock the lights were extinguished, and at sunrise we discovered that it had two masts and three smoke stacks, carried guns, and bore the name of *Desaix*. It was a French armoured cruiser. The other part of the dock revealed itself to be an Italian ship called *Juliana*. We had little desire to tie up at this dock, and so directed our course toward land.

Our chief concern now was that we might be discovered by the armoured cruiser that was not far distant. The rigging of one of my boats was Chinese, of the other three, German. Four gray boats rigged in this extraordinary fashion could not fail to attract attention. When we had come close enough to the shore, I anchored, and had the other three boats come alongside and made fast. Quickly our masts and rigging disappeared, and we held a consultation with regard to what it was now best to do. The *Choising* was gone. Behind us lay the French armoured cruiser and the Italian vessel.

What attitude Italy had assumed toward the war by this time was wholly unknown to me. Before us lay the land with the surf beating between us and it. The indications were that this part of Arabia was now in the hands of the French. To remain in the boats was not possible, as, in the course of the day, we would surely be seen by the Frenchmen who were now enjoying an early morning nap aboard the armoured cruiser. My orders therefore were: "Pull for the shore."

Fortunately our heavily laden boats got through the surf without either capsizing or filling. On our way to the shore we met a small Arabian boat whose sole occupant, an Arab, was engaged in fishing, and who in response to our questions gave us the comforting information that Hodeida was now in the hands of the French. The mistake may be ascribed to the fact that although we spoke excellent German, and the Arab had a fluent command of Arabic, we nevertheless failed to understand each other.

Just after our boats had passed through the surf and were about 800 metres off shore, they ran aground. All our belongings had therefore to be carried all this distance to land, and through water that was knee deep. Rafts were quickly put together out of the masts, a few boards, some straps, life preservers, and the like. On them we placed our machine guns, the ammunition, etc., so that the transportation might be made as rapidly as possible.

First of all, the machine guns were sent ashore. I waded to land along with them. On the beach an Arab was splashing about in the water. Unarmed, and with every expression of amiability and friendliness of which I am capable, I approached him to offer the hand of friendship. He misunderstood me, however, and departed. A second Arab, who had appeared in the meantime, was quite time, as unresponsive to my offers of friendship.

While I was employed in having the rest of our things put ashore, a man in uniform, and mounted on a *hedjin*, or riding camel, came toward me. The uniform was blue and red. Around his head a cloth was wound. To what country the uniform belonged, I had not the least idea. It might easily have been a French one. This man had the unpleasant distinction of being armed. When he had come to within 600 metres of us, he stopped, cocked his rifle, and stood watching us at our work. Carrying no arms of any kind, I went toward him, beckoned to him, called to him, and tried in every way possible to make him understand that I wished to speak with him. He remained immovable until I had come to within two hundred metres of him; then he raised his rifle and aimed it at me. I stood still. He lowered his rifle, whereupon I moved a few steps nearer.

Again he pointed his rifle at me. Again I stopped, and he dropped his rifle. Again I took a few steps forward, and again he aimed at me. I stopped again, and so the teasing performance went on for several minutes, until I had reached a point not more than fifty metres distant from him. Then his rifle was not again lowered. Consequently I remained standing for some time. An understanding by way of conversation was out of the question with him. He had not understood one of my efforts at speech. He made a sign, however, which could not be misinterpreted, and by which he gave me to understand that I was to remain with my men where we were. After I had assured him, as best I could, that we had no thought of leaving, and that we were delighted to be there, I returned to my men. He mounted his camel and disappeared at a rapid pace in the direction of Hodeida, the white houses of which we could but just distinguish in the far distance.

It now behooved us to make all haste possible, for in three or four hours the French garrison might be upon us. So we worked with all our might to get the things ashore, and so be able to start upon our march into the desert.

It was my intention to remain in the desert during the day, and then at night to send one of my officers to Hodeida to get information. Should this prove unfavourable, I purposed to spend the following day also in the desert, and then, on the next night, to get back to where the *Choising* would pick us up, and to proceed with her, trusting to luck for the future.

Just as we were about to set off on our march, there poured forth from behind the low sand hills of the desert a swarm of Bedouins,—at first about eighty in number, then a hundred or more, all armed. They spread out into a sort of skirmishing line, and then disappeared behind the sand dunes along the beach. Upon seeing this, we, too, formed a skirmishing line, and made ready for a fight. I waited for the first shot to come from the other side. After a few moments there came out from among our opponents twelve unarmed men.

They approached us slowly, all the while beckoning with their arms. Laying aside my sword and pistol, I went toward them. Midway between the two lines we met. Immediately a lively conversation developed, with the unfortunate disadvantage, however, that neither party understood the other. The Bedouins shouted at me, gesticulated violently with the vehemence peculiar to southern races, and made the most remarkable signs, all of which I failed to understand. My own attempt to speak to them in German, English, French, and Malay was of as little avail.

I then had our war flag, which we had with us, brought out, and I called attention in the most explicit manner to the red, white, and black, to the iron cross, to the eagle. They did not understand this either. As I had thought it quite likely that the people of some of the coast regions where we might be forced to land would be unacquainted with the German war flag, I had taken the flag of our merchant marine with me also. It was now produced and displayed to the Arabs, but this, too, they did not recognize. Then we pointed to the French armoured cruiser lying at anchor in the roadstead, shook our fists at it with the most extravagant gestures, and all together roared, "*Boom! Boom! Boom!*"

The only response we received was a return to their crazy signs.

One of these was to hold one hand to the forehead, as though to shade the eyes, and then wag the head violently from side to side. Another was to pass two fingers over the face, either up or down. A third consisted in rubbing the two extended forefingers together, and staring at us idiotically the while. This last one we thought we understood. We interpreted it in this way: Two are rubbing against each other, which means, "We are enemies." With all the means in our power we tried to assure them that quite the reverse was true. Had we been understood, our situation would hardly have been improved by this assurance, for it developed later that this sign meant, "We are friends," instead of, "We are enemies."

As a last resort, we produced a gold piece. To this means of intercourse the Arabians were very susceptible from the outset. We pointed at the eagle, but it did not seem to suggest anything to them. Then I pointed at the head of the *Kaiser*. This met with instant response, and aroused the liveliest interest. Among their ejaculations we distinguished the word, "*Aleman*." This was understood on our part, for it could mean nothing other than "German." Instantly, and with ready adaptability to the customs of the country, we all shouted at the top of our voices, "*Aleman! Aleman!*" And with this, the way to a mutual understanding was opened.

A tremendous and enthusiastic roar of response instantly arose among the Arabs. Their rifles were stacked, and the whole company gathered about us, screaming and shouting, and tumbling over one another in a wild scramble to carry our luggage for us, to drag the machine guns, and to do us other like service. In a tumult of noise the procession set out in the direction of Hodeida. One of our newly acquired brethren could even speak a few words of English, and from him I learned that Hodeida was in the hands of the Turks.

Our onward march was the occasion for still further excitement. As destitute of people as the desert through which we were passing seemed to be, it nevertheless harboured a countless number of people. In this land, where every boy of twelve carries a rifle and is regarded as a warrior, it did not take long for another crowd of about a hundred Bedouins to gather and come out to meet us, all eager, in the assumption that we were enemies, to have a shot at us. With much excited yelling, our hundred attendants endeavoured to convince their approaching hundred colleagues that we were friends. When they had been persuaded that such was the case, we continued on our march with a retinue of two hundred, only to be met, a half hour later, by two hundred more who were coming to attack us, and who, in turn, had to be convinced by our escort of two hundred, that we were friends.

These explanations always entailed a considerable loss of time, and so it had got to be midday, and we were still on the way. We had had nothing to eat since the evening before, had worked hard and continuously, and had taken a long tramp through the burning sand at a time of day when, under ordinary circumstances, even to ride abroad is avoided. All told, there were probably eight hundred Bedouins moving along with us. They had at last understood that we were Germans, and now carried on quite a variety show as they went along with us, dancing and singing, yelling and shooting off their rifles, and carrying on all sorts of fantastic performances.

In the meantime, the first Turkish officers from Hodeida had arrived, among them several who could speak German. Our mutual joy at meeting comrades in arms was great. The whole Turkish garrison of Hodeida was marching out against us in the belief that a detachment of the enemy was attempting a landing. Cannons even had been dragged along to assail us.

Surrounded by the Turkish troops, and with banners flying, we made our entry into Hodeida. The people filled the streets and shouted their welcome at us, and flattered us with loud cries of approval and a vigorous clapping of hands at the close of every marching song we sang as we moved along.

Hastily prepared barracks were soon made ready for my men. For the officers, a house in the town was provided. And so, for the present, we were comfortable. From the windows of our house we could see the French armoured cruiser peacefully and dreamily rocking upon the blue water a few miles off.

CHAPTER 10

On to Sanaa

At 5 o'clock in the afternoon of the ninth of January, my men were all settled in their quarters, and I found myself free to consult with the heads of the civil and military authorities at Hodeida with regard to my future course. There were two ways of getting back to Germany open to me: the one, overland, and the other, to continue on my way by sea. Marine charts I could obtain in Hodeida. His Excellency, the *Mutessarif* of Hodeida, whose name was Raghib, and the colonel of the regiment, also named Raghib, sat together in consultation with me that afternoon

I learned at once, and much to my regret, that the railroad did not exist. At the same time I received information with regard to the English warships then in the Red Sea. These consisted chiefly of a number of gunboats and auxiliary cruisers, that could be seen almost daily to the northward of Hodeida, and that were maintaining a sort of blockade line. To continue on the *Choising* under these circumstances was very nearly a hopeless undertaking, especially so in consideration of the probability that spies would very soon make our presence in Hodeida known abroad. The French iron-clad would surely hear of it, and could at once participate in the search for our ship, while her wireless apparatus could flash information of us to all the English and French war vessels in the vicinity. In waters as narrow as the Red Sea is, it would then be quite impossible for the *Choising*, with a speed of but seven miles, to elude her pursuers.

The Turkish authorities assured me, moreover, that I would find the overland route to the north both safe and unobstructed, although it would necessarily entail some loss of time. Preparations for the journey by land would require about a fortnight; then we could start on our march, and, in all likelihood, would reach the railroad in about two months.

When this was fully settled, I waited for the darkness to come, and then, from the roof of our house, three times I sent off the signal with fire balls, as agreed upon, to the waiting *Choising*: "Caution! Hostile ships! Proceed at once to Massowa." Later we learned that the *Choising* had reached her destination in safety.

Whereas the health of my men had been excellent up to this time, they now began to show the effects of the extreme climate. In Hodeida the days were terribly hot, the nights very cool. The men of our crew slept in the Turkish barracks along with the soldiers of the Turkish garrison.

In Arabia houses and barracks are constructed very differently from those in our own climate. The barracks provided for my men consisted of a framework of thin boards covered with matting and straw. They slept side by side on a sort of divan, the cushions of which were stuffed with straw. The water especially was unwholesome, and had to be boiled to make it fit to drink. As a preventive measure against malarial infection, we had to take quinine continuously. But in spite of all our precaution, cases of dysentery and malaria soon began to develop among us. I therefore decided to take my men into the mountains. Sanaa, which is the chief city of Yemen, was recommended to me as being a very healthful place, the water conditions good, and the climate closely resembling that of Europe. Since our journey overland lay by way of Sanaa, it was quite as well to await the completion of our preparations for it at that place as at Hodeida. I decided therefore to start on our march to Sanaa on the *Kaiser's* birthday.

Before leaving Hodeida we celebrated the anniversary of our Emperor's birth by ceremonies in which the entire Turkish garrison participated, as did also the entire Turko-Arabian populace, in their own peculiarly enthusiastic fashion. I had in the meantime succeeded in procuring new clothes for my men. Although this, their latest uniform, did not exactly conform to home regulations,—especially the tropical hat designed by myself after the pattern of the hats worn by the colonial troops, and decorated with a large cockade in red, white, and black, the like of which, it is safe to say, had never before been seen in the navy,—nevertheless the men presented a very trim appearance, and made an excellent impression.

The entire garrison marched to the parade square for the ceremony. My little company of men stood in the middle, surrounded by the Turkish troops. Together with the Turkish commander, I passed the combined troops in review; I then made a speech in German in honour of the *Kaiser*, and ended with three cheers for him, in which our Turkish comrades in arms joined with enthusiasm. After the cheers for our Emperor had been given, the Turkish commander called for three cheers for the *Sultan*. A parade march by the combined troops closed the ceremonies. With band playing and banners flying, my men then marched off to a feast—mutton and rice—spread for them in the barracks. The officers were invited by the heads of the local authorities to a banquet—mutton and rice—at the palace of the Mayor of Hodeida. Here, also, the heartiest good will was expressed in the toasts that were exchanged. At five o'clock in the afternoon we started on our march to Sanaa.

In the Arabian desert it is only possible to travel at night, as the heat of the day is too intense to be borne by either man or beast. Marching on foot is out of the question even at night. Everybody rides. We also had to follow this custom until we reached the foot of the mountains.

The animals placed at our disposal were horses, mules, and donkeys. Our baggage was transported by means of a special caravan of camels. It was no light task to keep this newly organized company together at the start, for this was the first time that some of my bluejackets had ever been astride of a four-footed creature. The fun began at once, with the mounting, and there were some very ludicrous scenes. Some of the men took advantage of the time before we started on the march, to practise rapid dismounting, many of them taking their saddles along with them in the attempt. However, relations of friendship sufficient to insure against the occurrence of any serious misunderstanding had soon been established between each rider and his mount, and the caravan was ready to start. We were escorted for some distance by the Turkish officers and garrison.

Soon Hodeida was left behind us in the distance, and we were in the heart of the desert. As far as the eye could reach, there was nothing but sand,—low flat sand hills grown over with dry grass. Roads, of course, there were none; tracks in the sand, made by the passing of other caravans,—that was all. Our march was frequently interrupted by a halt, for in the beginning especially, it happened every little while that one of the men devoted an over-amount of energy to guiding and mastering his steed, and the ensuing duel usually came off to the humiliation of the rider. The next thing to be done then, was to catch the riderless beast that was making the most of its freedom, a duty which usually devolved upon the officers, as they were the only ones who could ride. With the donkeys and the mules this was no small undertaking. Hardly had we come up to one of these animals when it would turn and kick out vigorously with its hind legs, and it would then require a resort to all the diplomacy and cunning at our command to get hold of it again. That these diversions should not cause us too great a loss of time, one of the officers always rode at the rear end of the caravan to round up the riderless steeds, and the steedless riders, and form them into a sort of rear guard.

As the nights were clear and bright with moonlight, we found our way very easily. We rode the whole night through, stopping only occasionally for a half hour's rest. Then we all flung ourselves down in the sand, just where we happened to be, slung our reins around one arm, or tied them to one of our legs, and so found rest for our weary bodies, weary from the strain of the long continued ride.

The region through which we were travelling was not considered a wholly safe one. Robbery and attacks upon small caravans were the order of the day. As early as the second night out, we had an experience of this kind ourselves. Suddenly, in the moonlight, there appeared to one side of our road a dozen or more men mounted on camels. The Turkish *gendarmes* that had been sent with us as an escort and to guide us on the way, declared them to be robbers, and immediately got their rifles ready to shoot. When the men on the camels saw the size of our caravan, they vanished among the sand hills quite as suddenly as they had appeared.

On the third day we had completed the journey across the broad strip of desert which lies at the foot of the mountains, and we were now at the entrance into the mountain region. Quite abruptly, almost perpendicularly, the mountains rise from out the flat desert country, and attain a height of some 3600 metres. The route now became more difficult. Over loose stones, through dry beds of rivers and brooks, we climbed slowly upward. At last we were again surrounded by trees and bushes, and the vegetation became quite luxuriant. On many of the highest peaks of the mountains Arab castles were to be seen. The Arabs of this region seem to delight in placing their dwellings on as great and inaccessible a height as possible. At every point where a steep cliff or a narrow defile makes the upward way a difficult one, some Arab had built him a castle, frequently large and imposing in appearance, a veritable little fortress in itself. It was almost as though we had suddenly been transported back into the Middle Ages.

The people were very friendly, and we met with a pleasant greeting everywhere. Our periods of rest were usually spent in the caravansaries provided for the Turkish troops. For some days our road lay through a picturesque mountain region, and then brought us directly in front of a lofty mountain ridge that seemed to block our way completely, so that we did not know which way to turn. It was a steep, well nigh perpendicular wall of rock. A serpentine path, most difficult to climb, brought us to the summit of the ridge, after hours of exertion. It was a road by no means free from danger. On the one side of us the wall of rock rose straight up; on the other side it dropped straight down. A road, in the ordinary sense of the word, it really was not. It was no more than a bridle path worn into the rock by many long years of travel, often blocked by a great boulder, and made dangerous with many rolling stones.

The pack animals showed a wonderful ability and power of endurance. Often we came to places so dangerous that I gave orders to dismount, and lead the animals. As a whole, however, the men had come to be quite good riders by this time. We bought eggs and milk on the way whenever we had an opportunity to do so. We carried our cooking utensils with us on one of the animals. An officer, the cook, and another man always preceded the caravan, as a small number of men can travel faster than a larger company. In this way our meals were always ready for us when we arrived at the appointed place. This was a distinct advantage for the men, for the journey was a very fatiguing one, and every hour of sleep was of importance.

I had arranged for a longer halt to be made at Menakha. This is a small town situated on the highest point of the principal mountain ridge. From thence the road winds gradually downward until it reaches an extensive plateau on which Sanaa is located. In Menakha we were given a pleasant welcome by both the Turkish troops and the people. At a point some hours distant from the little town, we found the commandant, together with his corps of officers and the troops, awaiting us. A crowd of several hundred people had come with them. Together with the Turkish soldiery, we covered the last part of the way to Menakha, while before us went the great crowd of picturesquely dressed Arabs carrying on a sort of performance, and dancing to the accompaniment of a peculiar kind of song.

Excellent provision had been made for us at Menakha. On account of the weather conditions here, the buildings are all of stone. My men found large barracks awaiting them in which every comfort had been

View of Hodeida

Crossing the desert

provided, and where an abundant and appetizing meal was in readiness. For the officers, accommodations had been prepared in the hotel of the town, the only hotel that I ever saw in Arabia. It could even boast of real beds. So far we had slept on "*cursis*," which consist of a wooden framework filled in with a matting of bast. Menakha lies at a height of about 3400 metres, and we often saw the clouds below us. The days were cool, and the nights were bitterly cold.

We remained in Menakha for two days. I took advantage of this time to visit a number of the Arab dignitaries in their homes. The rooms in all Arab houses are white throughout, while the windows are set with bright coloured glass—blue, red, and yellow. Along the walls are low comfortable divans and cushions. On the carpet, in the middle of the room, stands a large brass table on which are the *nargilehs*.[1] According to the customs of the country, we were always offered a cup of *Mocha* on these occasions, and we spent many a pleasant hour smoking and chatting as best we could with our Arab hosts.

From Menakha our way lay downward again. The Turks were improving the condition of their roadways here, and for some distance from the town we followed a fine, broad and newly made road leading down into the valley, a highway that compared favourably with any in Europe. Our journey now took us through some wonderful mountain scenery. To see camels grazing by the wayside, nibbling at the tops of low trees, never ceased to be a marvellous sight to us. Occasionally, too, we caught a glimpse of a lot of baboons, but never got a shot at one of them, as often as we tried it. By this time the horsemanship of my troop had improved to such a degree that we could maintain a very respectable formation, and now and again could even ride at an easy trot.

The seventh day of our journey found us approaching the capital city. From the heights, on our way through the passes, we could look down upon a wide and fruitful plateau, sprinkled with many villages and towns, among which Sanaa could readily be distinguished by its size. Turkish officers had ridden out to meet us. just outside of the city the whole garrison stood lined up, and received us with bands playing gaily. "*Deutschland, Deutschland ueber Alles*" greeted our ears. The heads of the civil and military authorities came on horseback or in carriages. The people also showed a lively interest in our arrival. Even the French consul, who was being detained in the city as a measure of retaliation, appeared on the balcony of his house. We had come in

1. Oriental water pipes.

contact with his English colleague on our way hither, although without meeting him face to face. It must have given him a shock of surprise suddenly to hear "The Watch on the Rhine" sung in his home in the heart of the Arabian mountains.

Unfortunately Sanaa was not as healthful a place as we had hoped to find it. Owing to its great altitude it is very cold there even during the daytime. It takes some time to get accustomed to the climate. A few days after our arrival, eighty *per cent* of my men were sick with the fever, and unfit to continue on the march. We suffered especially with sudden and severe attacks of cramps in the stomach, and with colds.

The city of Sanaa is a most interesting one. It is divided into three sections,—the Jewish, the Arab, and the Turkish quarters. The city is entirely surrounded by brick walls, and is so built as to form a fortress. Within this fortress the three quarters of the town constitute three distinct fortresses, each enclosed within its own wall, and within each of these, every individual home is itself a distinct little fortress. All the streets and roads are enclosed within high walls, and are so laid out that, like our trenches, they can be swept throughout their entire length by rifle fire from certain vantage points.

The reason for building the towns in this peculiar fashion is to be found in the very unsafe conditions that prevail. Yemen has always had the reputation of being the most turbulent of the Turkish provinces, and in past years violent encounters between the Arabs and the Turks were the order of the day. Frequently these were of so serious a nature that the towns were besieged by garrisons. Sanaa, also, had been starved into surrender to the Arabs only a decade ago. Since that time, however, peace and quiet have reigned in the land.

After a fortnight spent in Sanaa, we learned that the difficulties of the journey overland were so great, that, after all, it would be impossible for me to get my men safely through by this route. The sickness among them compelled me to remain another fortnight in idleness. By that time, though still weak, the sick had so far recovered as to be able to ride their animals.

So we started on our return journey to Hodeida, there again to entrust ourselves to the sea.

Chapter 11

Shipwreck

Our return to Sanaa was accomplished in the same manner as we had travelled thither, and without hindrance of any kind. In order to make arrangements for our onward journey by sea, I had taken a few of my men with me and hurried on ahead of the caravan. In this way I succeeded in getting to Hodeida a day and a half ahead of the others. It took the caravan eight days to get there. To be sure, our little advance guard had spent both day and night in the saddle, the only halts being made when we changed animals.

As the *Choising* had been sent on, and there was nothing in the way of steamboats to be had at Hodeida, there was but one thing left for us to do,—to continue our journey in *zambuks*. A *zambuk* is a small sailboat much in use all along the Arabian coast, and is provided with a *dhow* sail.

I procured two such boats in Hodeida, each about fourteen metres long and four metres wide. These two *zambuks* I sent to Yabana, a little bay to the north of Hodeida. Because of the French armoured cruiser, still sleepily rocking at anchor, a departure from the harbour of Hodeida was out of the question for me. The Frenchman might accidentally have a spell of wakefulness. As I was aware that the country was swarming with English and French spies, I took pains to spread abroad the report that it was our intention to sail from Isa Bay on the thirteenth of March. It happened just as I had foreseen. On the afternoon of the twelfth of March the little and out-of-the-way Isa Bay, where no house, nor tree, nor bush is to be seen, and where there is hardly any water, was honoured for the first time since the beginning of the war by the presence of an English gunboat, which hunted for us with its searchlight all up and down the shore. The poor fellows! How they must have wondered where we were!

On the fourteenth of March, at five o'clock in the afternoon, my fleet sailed from Yabana. The Imperial war flag flew proudly at the mast-head of my flagship, and with three cheers for his Majesty, the Emperor, we began our onward journey. The flagship of the second admiral was in command of Lieutenant Gerdts. We made up for the total lack of any further ships in the fleet by our absolutely correct discipline. As the second *zambuk* was somewhat larger than mine, the sick were put aboard of it. Malaria, dysentery, and typhus were still prevalent among the men, of whom there were always one or two so ill as to cause us the gravest anxiety. Under no circumstances, however, would I have been willing to leave any of them behind, for their only hope of improvement lay in a change of climate.

With regard to the English I had kept myself posted up to the last minute as best I could, and I was aware that an English blockade was being maintained by two gunboats together with the auxiliary cruiser *Empress of Russia*, in a line extending from Loheia across Kamaran, Jebel Sebejir to Jebel Soghair. My problem now was how I could run this blockade with my sailboats. To avoid the possibility of both boats being captured at the same time, I gave Lieutenant Gerdts orders to separate from me. A meeting place farther to the north was appointed, where we were to wait a while for each other.

Soon the other *zambuk* was lost to sight in the darkness of the approaching night. Now, for the first time, our lucky star forsook us, for, as the day dawned, the wind died away entirely, and, after the sun had risen, we discovered to our extreme discomfiture that we were exactly where we had no wish to be, namely, right in the middle of the English blockade line. We expected at any moment to see the mast-head of an English ship appear above the horizon. Our frame of mind was not of the happiest. The absence of wind detained us more surely than the most superior of foes could have held us. But it had not been without a good reason that I had delayed our departure to the end of the week. I was sufficiently familiar with English customs to know that the gentlemen are disinclined to work during weekends, that is, on Saturdays and Sundays. And nothing did, in fact, come in sight during the entire day.

The breeze, which set in during the course of the afternoon, helped us onward considerably, and by evening, soon after sunset, we could go to rest with the comfortable assurance that with two sailboats, and making but little headway, we had succeeded in running the English blockade.

With my flat-bottomed *zambuks* it was possible for me to shape my further course so as to keep within the coral reefs of the Farsan Bank. This is a dangerous and very long coral bank having an extent of about three hundred and fifty nautical miles, and near which large ships dare not venture. It is not wholly free from danger even for small craft. In the course of the following day, my second *zambuk* came in sight, and received orders to keep by me.

Life on the *zambuks* was rather pleasant and quite cosy. An abundance of room we did not have, of course. Including the interpreter, the pilot, and the Arabs we had taken with us for service with the sails and the ships, we numbered thirty-five men to each *zambuk*. With a length of fourteen metres, and a width of four, it can be readily seen that but little space could be allotted to each man. Moreover, a large part of each boat had to be devoted to the storing of provisions, water, ammunition, and the machine guns. To protect ourselves, in a measure at least, from the burning rays of the sun, we stretched woollen blankets across the ship so as to be able to keep our heads in the shade. Our culinary department was not run on a lavish scale. In each *zambuk* there was a small open fireplace lined with tin. Here the meals for thirty persons had to be cooked. We tried to make our meals as varied as possible with the limited means at our disposal. Thus, for instance, if we had tough mutton with rice and gravy on one day, we would have rice with gravy and tough mutton on the next, and on the third day, there would be gravy with tough mutton and rice, and so on.

Our boats made but very slow progress. Oftentimes we were becalmed, and there were frequent struggles with head winds and opposing currents. Nor were these troubles from without our only ones, for there were conflicts within our boat as well. These raged most fiercely at night, for then the cockroaches, bedbugs, and lice were especially active. All articles of clothing that were not in use had to be tied fast to something for fear they might run away. In the morning, as soon as the sun was up, every man of us pulled off his shirt, and the general "early louse hunt" was begun. The record number for one shirt was seventy-four.

On the seventeenth of March I signalled to my fleet: "I intend to anchor in the evening." According to our pilot, we were getting into a vicinity where the reefs made it unsafe even for our small craft to sail at night. By six o'clock in the evening we were drawing near to the island of Marka, where we were to anchor. Our pilot was conducting us to our anchorage. My *zambuk* led the way. The second one followed at a distance of two hundred metres. There was a pretty stiff breeze blowing, with correspondingly high seas, and we were looking forward with eagerness to getting a little rest in the lee of the sheltering island. But we had made our reckoning without our host in the person of our capable Arab pilot. He directed our course so skilfully that my boat suddenly struck a coral reef. A second and a third time she pounded so hard that I had grave fears for the safety of the boat.

The next moment we were free of the reef, however, and in deeper water. I dropped anchor at once. Then, in order to keep the boat behind us from running aground upon the same reef, I quickly gave her captain orders by signs and shouts to hold off. This he did, but his boat was already so in the midst of the reefs that, in the endeavour to avoid one reef, he struck another. In a moment more I saw a flag run up, a sign that something had happened. The next instant the boat dipped slowly. From the motion of the mast, I knew that the boat was pounding. Suddenly it disappeared,—only the top of the mast could be seen rising on a slant out of the water. It was now just before sundown.

Night sets in very suddenly in these southern latitudes. Ten minutes after the sun has set, it is absolutely dark. There was no moon at the time. Instant help was therefore necessary. Up went the sail on our *zambuk*. All hands set to work. The anchor was pulled up, and by a difficult manoeuvre in which we came near running aground again, we got away, and hastened to the relief of our comrades. I took my boat as close to the submerged *zambuk* as possible, and cast anchor again. But on account of the reef I was obliged to keep at a distance of four hundred metres. We had no small boats that we could send back and forth. Each *zambuk* carries but a single dugout,—a very small and narrow paddle boat, made from a single tree trunk, and capable of carrying no more than two men at the most. With the high seas running at the time, their usefulness was a matter of doubt. Nevertheless I sent mine out at once.

In the meantime it had grown dark. We had a lantern aboard our *zambuk*, but all the many attempts we made to light it, in order to show our ship's position, failed, as the strong wind that was blowing extinguished the light again and again. "Torchlights!" was my next order. We had taken with us a few torches from both the *Emden* and the *Choising* for possible cases of emergency. These were now brought out and nailed up. The fuses worked all right, but the torches refused to burn. They had grown too damp in the many months that we had carried them about with us.

Suddenly, out of the darkness of the night, I heard voices rising from the water just behind us. The first men from the foundered *zambuk* had reached us, and, unable to see us in the darkness, they were swimming past us. By shouting, by whistling with the boatswain's whistle, we tried to call them back, and, after some anxious moments, we succeeded in doing so. The men had swum away from the other *zambuk*, and, having nothing else to guide them, they had followed a star that shone down from the direction of our boat. How many of the men were in the water we had, of course, no means of knowing. My anxiety for them was great, knowing, as I did, that the water in this vicinity is full of sharks.

My greatest concern, however, was for the sick, and I wondered what had been done for them, for many of them were too weak to help themselves. That which was needed above all else now, was for us to show a light. As every other means had failed us, I had the men bring wood, pile it together, pour petroleum on it, and, with little care for the danger we ran of setting our boat afire, we set it in a blaze. In the fire thus kindled, we held our torches until they were dry enough to burn. At the same time we set off a few white fire balls that we had with us, and which, thank God, were still in good condition, although by firing off these rockets, we revealed our presence to other ships for miles about.

At last the two dugouts returned. They were rowed by one man, and in each one lay one of the sick. The others who were too ill to do anything for themselves were either brought aboard our boat in the same way, or else they were tied to one of the dugouts, and towed along in the water. Meanwhile, all those who could swim were arriving from every side. The men who could not swim—and there were a number such—had put on life-preservers, and were paddling along as best they could. One after another they came aboard. Soon there were fifty of us in my little *zambuk*, and then it settled so low in the water that it was evident it would hold no more. I therefore ordered everything that could possibly be spared, including provisions and water, to be thrown overboard, in order to lighten the boat sufficiently to carry us all. Finally, all that was left us was our arms, ammunition, and food and water sufficient for three days.

In the meantime our torches had burned low, and I was filled with anxiety lest their light would not hold out until the last man from the wrecked *zambuk* had come aboard. At last all were accounted for except the officers, and, with the arrival of the last one of these, the last torch died out. So, for the present at least, all were safe. The wrecked *zambuk*, according to the reports of the officers in command of it, lay hard aground on an abruptly descending coral reef, and we had reason to be grateful that at least the mast had remained above water. It might have happened quite as well that the *zambuk* had slipped down the side of the reef, and vanished in the deep. In that case all the sick would surely have been lost, and most likely some of the men who could not swim would also have been drowned.

Near us lay another *zambuk*, which belonged to the Idriss tribe. The Idriss are an Arab race that is not very friendly to the Turks, and is especially averse to European influence of any kind. From this *zambuk* a canoe had been sent to the rescue when my second *zambuk* stranded. But as soon as it was discovered that we were Europeans—a circumstance which was revealed by the tropical hat worn by our doctor—the canoe turned back, and left our men to their fate. To continue our journey in my one greatly overladen boat was a very precarious undertaking,—there were now some seventy persons aboard of her—and especially so in consideration of the very meagre supply of provisions we had with us.

Therefore, just before sunrise, I sent our Arab interpreter to the Idriss *zambuk* to offer those in charge of it a large sum of money for the use of their boat for a few days. They refused my offer flatly, however, saying that, should I offer them a hundred thousand pounds, they would do nothing for dogs of Christians. It would, of course, have been an easy matter for me to have made myself master of the desired *zambuk* by force, and, indeed, it had been my intention to do so as soon as it should be fully day. I was very averse to such a proceeding, however. It might have had some very unpleasant consequences politically, for it involved the use of armed force against allies, even though these allies were but a race of wild and uncivilized people.

But the day brought us better fortune; our lucky star was once more in the ascendant. A stiff southerly breeze was blowing, which made it possible for me to sail even with my overloaded boat, as I could run before the wind. It gave us the promise of rapid progress during the day. So I left the Idriss boat in peace.

We now hurried to save what we could from the wrecked *zambuk*. We wanted most of all to recover our arms. The *zambuk* had sunk still lower during the night. The mast was broken off, and the ship lay on the bottom, tilted downward. By diving, we succeeded in recovering the two machine guns, a few pistols, and a part of the ammunition.

Everything else, our provisions, our clothing, and the like, was lost, and, unfortunately, our entire medical outfit as well.

The stiff breeze from the south carried us in a single afternoon over a distance which it would have taken us about six days to cover under the previously existing conditions.

By evening we had arrived at Coonfidah. Here we were given a most friendly welcome. As there had been no opportunity to make special preparation for our coming, a genuine Turkish meal was quickly made ready for us, and we ate it according to the local custom, without the use of plates, forks, or knives. A whole sheep, boiled and stuffed with rice, was placed on the table. With eager hands we set to work to denude the bones of the meat that was on them, and with our fingers we put the rice into our mouths. At Coonfidah we met a Turkish government official and his wife, who were also on their way to Constantinople, and who became our travelling companions. In the further course of our journey this official rendered me good service as dragoman, that is, as interpreter.

It was our good fortune to find a large *zambuk* while we were in Coonfidah. We chartered it, and so were enabled to continue our journey all together in one boat. Without meeting with further difficulties of any kind, we reached Leet on the afternoon of the twenty-fourth day of March. This town marks the northern extremity of the Farisan Bank, between the coral reefs of which we had so far found safety from pursuit by our English foes. Our further course by water would now take us out into the open sea. It was evident that the English would do all in their power to capture us there. While in Leet, chance placed in my hands a letter that had come from a merchant in Djidda. He wrote that Djidda was closely blockaded by English warships, and that not even a *zambuk* was allowed to enter the harbour without inspection by the English.

This prohibited our further journey by sea. There was therefore but one way open to us, and that lay overland. We remained in Leet two days, just long enough to get together the animals needed for our caravan, to provide ourselves with the required amount of water, and to make all other necessary preparations for our onward march.

In Leet occurred the first death in our number. One of our seamen, Keil, had been suffering from a severe attack of typhus ever since our sojourn at Hodeida. The hardships of the shipwreck had proved too much for his already exhausted body, and, as our medical stores had all been lost, we could not even give him medical aid as we journeyed on. He died on the twenty-seventh of March, at three o'clock in the morning. Two of his comrades watched at his bier, as they had at his bedside throughout his illness. We made a row-boat ready, sewed the body in sailcloth, and weighted it with stones. The war flag was then draped over it, and on this was laid the hat and bared sword of the dead. After a brief religious service, we laid the body of our comrade in the boat, and, taking it out to where the water was deep, we committed it to its last resting place. Three volleys resounded over his watery grave. We did not deem it wise to give our dead a burial on land, as, in all likelihood, the wild and fanatical people of the country would have disturbed his last sleep.

On the twenty-eighth of March we began our onward journey.

Chapter 12

The Attack

It did not prove an altogether easy task to collect in Leet all the camels that we needed for our journey. Leet is a very small town with a population numbering only a few hundred, and with no commercial connections whatever. To facilitate matters with regard to our journey I thought it advisable to pay my respects to the Sheikh of Leet. Never before had a Christian entered his home.

The medium of our conversation was my *dragoman*. After the customary felicitations had been exchanged, the Sheikh invited me to dine with him. His house was a hut put together of boards and matting, and without windows of any kind. Along two sides of the room stood divans covered with skins. The walls were hung with weapons. The rest of the furniture of the room consisted of smoking apparatus. Throughout the entire time before dinner, cups of *Mocha* and of a sort of lemonade were passed around. The coffee was of the Arabian variety, *viz.*, in its preparation the husks of the coffee bean, and not the beans themselves, are boiled. The result is a bitter drink not at all palatable to Europeans, but which, for the sake of politeness, must be swallowed down under any circumstances. The preparations for the meal were begun while we were sitting in the room.

First of all, quite a large round mat of woven straw was laid on the bare earth in the middle of the room. Then servants brought in rice, which was heaped in a huge mound in the middle of the mat. A few jars of mixed pickles completed the course. Instead of sitting, we lay down at the table. Spoons were provided, however. Soon we were all cheerfully doing our best to diminish the mountain of rice. Meanwhile the meat course had arrived at the front of the house. It consisted of a whole roast sheep, which, as such, did not make its appearance on the table however. Knives and forks there were none. Two servants, detailed for this special duty, tore the roast sheep into pieces with their hands, and placed before each one of us, on the mat, the piece that was intended for him.

In the course of the two days that we had to spend in Leet, we succeeded in getting together about ninety camels. With this number we could begin our march. The Sheikh assured us that we would meet with the others *en route* on the following day. I purchased a large number of straw mats and distributed them among my men. Later, these mats proved an excellent protection against the heat of the sun. Our caravan left Leet in the evening, and we began our march into the desert. Most of the camels carried only burdens, especially water, ammunition, the machine guns, and provisions. The water prospects for our journey were far from favourable. I had to reckon with the possibility of travelling for days without being able to replenish our water supply.

A journey on camels is necessarily a slow one. To begin with, the camel is not a speedy traveller; furthermore, ours was a caravan of ninety camels at the start, and later, of one hundred and ten. The camels on which the officers rode were the only ones that were allowed to run free. All the others were fastened together by ropes, the muzzle of one being tied by a rope of about four metres' length to the tail of the one in front of it. Naturally, the long line of camels thus formed could not move with the rapidity of a single animal, since the rate of progress of the whole line had to be kept down to the pace of the slowest camel. Moreover, frequent halts had to be made, to re-adjust packs that had slipped, to mend a broken saddle girth, to recover a saddle that had slipped off, and for other like causes of delay.

We kept to a route that follows the coast, close by the sea. This entire region is considered unsafe, robbery and attacks upon passing caravans being the order of the day. From the time we left Leet, our rifles were therefore kept loaded, and ready to shoot. We were fortunate in that the nights were bright with the light of a full moon. As a rule, we began the day's march at four o'clock in the afternoon, and arrived at nine or ten in the morning at the place where we were to rest. On an average, we spent about fourteen to eighteen hours a day in the saddle. As camels are pacers, it is very fatiguing to ride them.

The water places that we passed were mere holes dug into the sand of the desert, and were from fourteen to eighteen metres deep. With leather bags, which we lowered into them, we dipped up the water. The word water, in its European sense, is a misnomer, however, for this evil-smelling, brown or black, thick fluid, swarming with insects. At the bottom of some of the water holes a dead dog or sheep could be seen. To use it unboiled was therefore utterly out of the question. It frequently had a brackish taste also.

From Leet out, we were escorted by a Turkish officer and seven *gendarmes*. In addition, we were always accompanied by the sheikh of the district through which we happened to be passing, for it is customary in these parts to take with one, as hostage, the person who is responsible for the safety of the country. Such precautions are not looked upon as being anything unusual here. In this way our march proceeded without interruption of any kind until the thirty-first day of March.

At about eleven o'clock on the morning of this day, we arrived at a watering place which is but a day's march distant from Djidda, our next objective point. At this water hole we found an officer and seventeen *gendarmes*, who had been sent from Djidda to meet us and to bring us the greetings of our Turkish allies and of the civil authorities of Djidda. They had also brought us a liberal supply of water. We camped at the water hole as usual, stretched our straw mats and woollen blankets over the low thorny desert growth, and crawled under them far enough to find protection for our heads at least from the scorching heat of the sun.

The cooking was always the first thing undertaken after we had settled down. Dry wood was gathered along the way by all of the men, and so a fire was quickly started. On it our usual meal of rice and, if we were lucky, of mutton, was soon prepared.

When I saw the men who had been sent out from Djidda to meet us, I supposed that the most dangerous part of our journey was behind us. We were now getting into the vicinity of a town in which there was stationed a Turkish garrison of about three hundred men, and I said to myself that if seventeen men could come through unmolested from Djidda to us, then surely we, a company of fifty men, would be able to travel the same road to Djidda in safety.

This district is inhabited by a tribe that is composed wholly of direct descendants of the Prophet, but which nevertheless is notorious for its uncivilized ways, and its robberies. "Father of the Wolf" is the very appropriate name by which this part of the country is known.

As usual, we began our onward march at four o'clock in the afternoon. Our road now led us somewhat away from the sea. The country round about consists wholly of flat sand drifts. Nowhere can one see

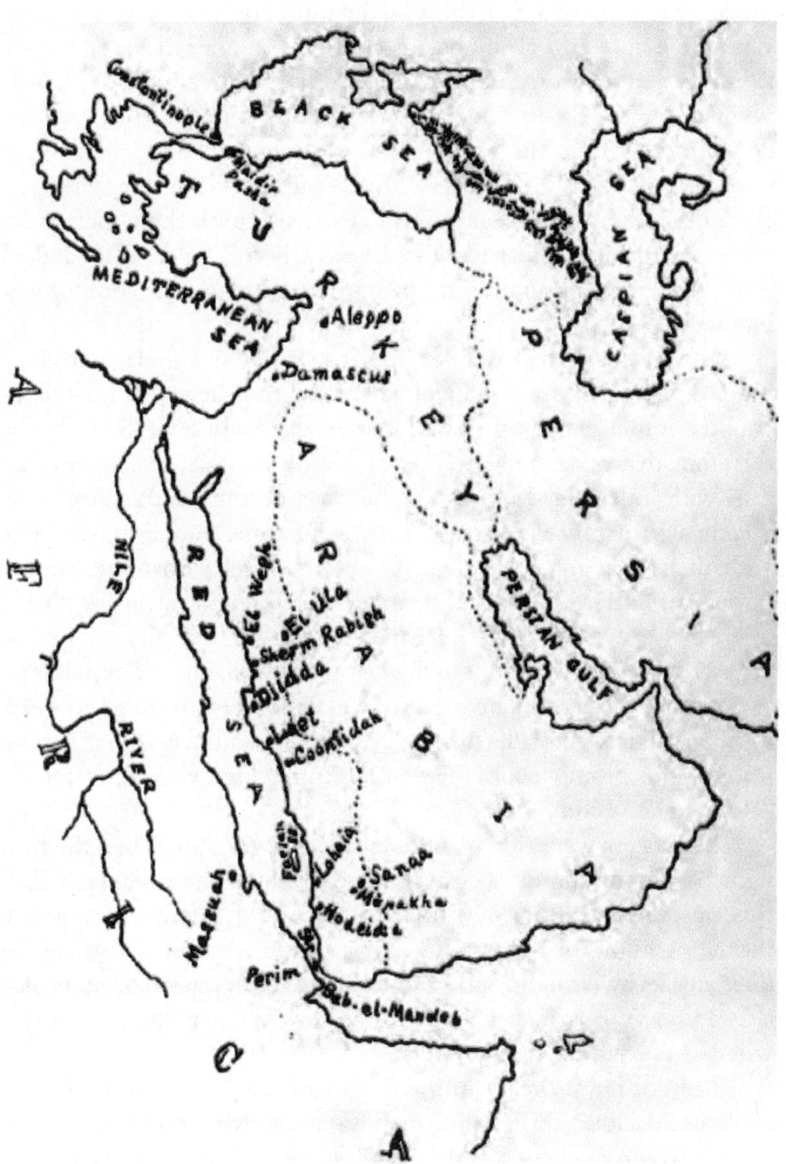

Constantinople
BLACK SEA
Haidir Pasha
TURKEY
MEDITERRANEAN SEA
Aleppo
Damascus
CASPIAN SEA
PERSIA
PERSIAN GULF
ARABIA
El Weph
El Ula
Sherm Rabigh
Djidda
Leet
Coonfidah
Lohaia
Sanaa
Menakha
Hodeida
RED SEA
NILE RIVER
Massuah
Perim
Bab-el-Mandeb
AFRICA

farther ahead than a distance of about four hundred metres. Hardly has one sand hill been passed, before another looms up to shut out the view. The drifts are overgrown with tufts of grass attaining a height of about two feet. We were trotting slowly along in the moonlight when suddenly, to our right, from beyond the usual course followed by caravans, there appeared a number of Bedouins, about twelve or fifteen, riding in a quick trot, and then vanished in the direction from which we had come. This looked rather suspicious, for, as a rule, caravans do not depart from the routes that have been trodden for thousands of years. Still less is it customary to ride off into the desert at a quick trot in the night-time. Our Turkish escort also took these men to be robbers, and told us that there had been talk in Djidda of a band of robbers, numbering about forty, by which this part of the country was infested.

As from Leet I had notified the authorities at Djidda, as well as those at Mecca, of our coming, I had reason to believe that the whole country round about was aware of our approach. Everybody knew, therefore, that our company was not one of the usual merchant caravans with little armed protection, but that, on the contrary, we were a company of fifty well-armed men, who were, moreover, carrying with them four machine guns. A rumour of forty roaming bandits caused me little disturbance of mind, therefore. Nevertheless, that I might have my men better in hand, and be prepared for any emergency, I took the precaution to divide our one long line of camels into two lines of fifty each. The men were given orders not to go to sleep on their camels, the rifles were all examined, and everything was in readiness for prompt action. The orders to my men were, once for all: "Rally to your commander."

The officers were riding at the head of the caravan. When the first signs of the coming day began to appear behind the mountains that rose on our right, from out the flat surface of the desert, I supposed that all occasion for anxiety was now passed, as Bedouins never make their attacks by daylight. So I slung my rifle across my saddle, unbuckled my heavy cartridge belt, and rode slowly down the line to see whether everything was in order.

I had got no farther than the middle of the caravan when I suddenly heard a loud, shrill whistle that was instantly followed by a volley of rifle fire. From every side it rained lead into our caravan incessantly, and at close range. The hum and whistle of the bullets made such a noise that the commands I shouted could not be heard. I grabbed my rifle, held it high, jumped from my camel, and, followed by my men, ran to the head of the caravan. Here the firing from both sides was well under way. From out the dusk of the early morning came the flash of the enemy's shots at a distance of about eighty metres. The riflemen themselves we could not see, any more than they could probably see us, when we lay on the ground. The tall forms of the camels, on the other hand, must have been quite visible to the enemy, and it was at these, most likely, that their fire was chiefly directed. The only guide to the position of our foes was the flash of their shots. As we were being fired at from every side, it was difficult to decide in which direction to turn first.

The larger number of my men was with me at the front. A few of them had been given orders to remain with the rear of the caravan.

The most important thing for us to do now was to get our most effective weapons, the machine guns, into play. Of these, two were strapped on camels at the head of the caravan, and two at the rear. In a few minutes we had the machine guns in action, and hardly had their volleys rattled over the enemy's lines, when silence reigned there. This turn in affairs had evidently not been expected. We took advantage of this lull in the enemy's fire to pull down the camels that were still standing, so that they would not form so easy a target, to distribute ammunition, and to get together.

The heaviest fire had poured down upon us from forward to the left, and it was therefore in this direction that I now led my men. Our equipment of firearms consisted, all told, of the four machine guns, thirteen German, and three modern Turkish rifles, together with ten old Turkish rifles that I had secured in Coonfidah to replace those lost with the wrecked *zambuk*. Of these, the three modern Turkish rifles had been distributed among the officers. In addition, we had twenty-four pistols among us, which, however, could only be of service in an encounter at close range. What the strength of the enemy was, we could not tell as yet. There might be from sixty to eighty men firing rapidly, or there might be many more who fired slowly. Their number was soon to be revealed to us by the coming day. When it was fully light, we could see that within our immediate vicinity the sand hills were black with Bedouins.

My men behaved splendidly. Not one of them showed the least perturbation in spite of the overwhelming superiority in numbers shown by the enemy, of whom there must have been at least three hundred. With one accord the bayonets appeared on all the rifles, although no order to that effect had been given.

During a moment of hesitation at the very outset of the firing, which had now begun in good earnest, and before I had fully decided what it was best to do, the answer to my question came from the man at my right, who called to me.

"Well, what is it?" I asked.

"How soon are we going at it, sir?"

"At what?" was my question in reply.

"Why, at storming the enemy," came the answer from this eighteen-year-old boy.

"Exactly, my man! You're right. Up! March, march!"

With a hearty cheer we were up, and rushing the enemy's line. No doubt, such tactics were a novelty to Bedouins used to attacking a caravan. At any rate, the enemy's fire ceased almost entirely. As our shining bayonets came closer to our foes, they quickly took to flight, followed by our rifle fire, which visibly thinned their ranks. First, we stormed to our left, then to the front, and then to the right.

It was not necessary to follow the same tactics to the rear, as there the enemy had disappeared entirely.

As a result, the narrow circle within which we had been hemmed in by the enemy, had now been widened to one of about 1200 metres' distance from us. The firing had stopped altogether. I now assembled my men close by the caravan. The machine guns remained in position, in readiness to keep off the enemy, as well as to attack them.

In spite of the close range at which the shots had poured in upon us, we had, thank God, only one man wounded among the Germans of my company. A little surprise was in store for me, however, when I looked about me for my friends of the Arab escort. There is a German saying which runs, "He counts his dear ones that are present, to find his six increased to seven." In my case the situation was reversed. Instead of twenty-four *gendarmes*, we now had only seven. There were no dead. The missing were found when we reached Djidda.

Nearly all of the Arabs we still had with us had been shot in the leg. This was to be accounted for by the circumstance that, instead of advancing toward the enemy, they had run to cover among the camels. My men, who had lain in the sand some thirty to forty metres distant from the camels, had escaped the enemy's fire, which had passed over them. Our foes had aimed at the camels, and so, before our Arabs could pull the animals to their knees, to find complete shelter behind them, the enemy's bullets, in passing between the legs of the camels, had found a mark in the limbs of the heroes who had sought refuge there.

Of the enemy's losses we knew nothing at all. But, as we stormed past the evacuated positions where they had lain, we counted fifteen dead. It is the custom with Bedouins immediately to remove all weapons from the bodies of their fallen comrades. As such had been the case with all but one of the dead, only one of their rifles fell into our hands. It was a breech loader of the most modern English construction, and was gratefully added to our own equipment. All the distant sand hills were still full of Bedouins, as we could see. In so far as possible, each one of those who showed themselves within range of our rifle fire, received his share of it, the moral effect produced being the principal object in view for the time being.

We could not very well remain lying in the place where we were. I had at first thought that we were dealing with a band of brigands, whose purpose was the usual one, to capture the valuables we had with us. I had therefore come to the conclusion that our assailants, who had suffered considerable loss, had now thought better of their undertaking and had abandoned it.

Quite a number of our camels had been shot. We took from their packs everything that was most necessary to us, water especially, and, discarding all the less useful things from the burdens of the uninjured camels, replaced them with the indispensables.

I decided to leave the road usually travelled, and turn sharply to the left in the direction of the sea, which I saw shimmering in the distance. If we could reach it, it would afford us protection on one side, leaving us free to face our foes in front and at our rear. It was unfortunate that I could not make use of the machine guns while on the march. Having no limbers with us, the guns had to be carried by camels while we were on the march. To make the caravan more compact, it was divided into from four to six lines, which travelled abreast. The wounded were so placed on the camels that they hung on one side of the animal, which thus afforded them some protection against the flying bullets. Two of the four camels that carried machine guns were placed at the head of the caravan, and the other two at the rear.

An advance guard of ten men in a widely extended skirmish line was sent out about one hundred and fifty metres ahead of the caravan, while a like number of men formed a rear guard at the same distance from it. As there were only nine more men who carried rifles, these formed a protecting guard, as best they could, for the two wings. The men who were armed with pistols only, and so could take part in no engagement except one at close range, remained near the caravan. Lieutenant Gerdts was placed in command of the advance guard, Lieutenant Schmidt of the rear guard, and Lieutenant Gyssling, of the flanks. Lieutenant Wellmann had charge of the caravan itself, where Dr. Lang was also with the sick.

Slowly our company set forth, our flag carried before us. Our hope, that the enemy would not trouble us again, was not to be realized. We had hardly been ten minutes on the march when shots again poured in upon us from every side. There was scarce a sign of our foes to be seen. Their every movement at any distance of more than four hundred metres was completely hidden by the sand hills. Ten to twenty dark heads popping up with lightning rapidity from behind a sand hill here or there, was all that we could see. Their appearance was always followed the next instant by a volley of shot rattling about the caravan, and before we could get the slightest opportunity to return the fire, the heads had disappeared, and a shower of lead fell upon us from another direction.

At first, strange to say, not one of our number was hit, although the enemy's fire was so incessant that shots were constantly falling about us, little pillars of sand marking the spot where they struck, while sand and gravel was constantly flying in our faces. In a short time it became evident that the greatest pressure was being brought to bear upon our rear guard. At that end of the caravan the men had to turn every few minutes to silence the enemy by a vigorous return of their fire.

I was with the rear guard when a signal came from the front, reporting that strong hostile forces had come in sight in the direction toward which the caravan was moving. When I arrived at the front, I saw that the whole horizon was black with Bedouins. At the same time came the report from the rear that one of the camels carrying the machine guns had been shot. The rear guard had halted, to protect the gun, and Lieutenant Schmidt asked that fresh camels be sent to the rear, so that he might shift the dead camel's load. I now heard the machine guns of the rear guard firing. They had been unstrapped, set up, and brought into action.

I now ordered the caravan to halt, an order which was by no means easy to carry out, however, as most of the camel drivers had taken advantage of the darkness to disappear along with the Arab *gendarmes* at the beginning of the fight. While on my way back to the rear guard, the report reached me that seaman Rademacher had fallen, and that

Lieutenant Schmidt was mortally wounded, shot through the breast and abdomen. In the meantime the command of the rear guard had devolved upon Lieutenant Wellmann, who had brought with him two camels from the caravan, for the transport of the machine guns.

During our halt, the enemy's fire increased in severity, and a vigorous engagement was soon in progress. Suddenly the firing ceased altogether, and, as I looked about me for the cause, I saw two of the Arab *gendarmes*, who had remained with us, running toward the enemy's lines, waving large white cloths as they ran. At the same time a third *gendarme* came to tell me that his comrades wished to parley with the other side. Although this turn in affairs was in no way of my choosing, it was nevertheless a welcome one, for it had now become evident that this was no attack by a mere band of robbers, but one that was thoroughly organized.

As our assailants outnumbered us by at least ten to one, it would have been folly to continue our march at the slow gait of a camel's pace, on an open plain, under continued fire from the enemy. Moreover, my most effective weapon of defence, the machine guns, could not be used while on the march. Nor could our twenty-nine rifles be employed to the best advantage, as there were too few of us to make their fire effective in all the directions from which we would be attacked. In the long run, we would have been shot down one after the other.

We therefore took advantage of the pause in the battle, to fortify ourselves. Hastily we constructed defence works out of camel saddles, which we filled with sand, out of sacks of coffee, rice and other provisions. We strengthened the rampart thus formed by filling it about with sand, as best we could. The camels were placed all together in the middle of the enclosed space, and loop holes were quickly got ready. For want of better material, they were put together out of tin plates and side arms. As all this was done in great haste, our constructions were, of course, but temporary and incomplete. Our water bottles were quickly buried deep in the sand, where they were least likely to be damaged by the enemy's fire. Within our outer rampart we raised another little fortress, the walls of which were about one metre and a half high, and constructed of empty petroleum cans which we filled with sand. Here were placed the sick who were unfit for duty, the wounded, and the doctor.

As we had to reckon with the possibility of being fired upon from all sides, and our rampart afforded us protection in front only, the camels were so placed as to shelter us from the enemy's fire at the flanks and rear. For our severely wounded, Lieutenant Schmidt, we made a stretcher of rifles and a woollen blanket, on which he was carefully carried to the inner fortress. The seaman, who had fallen, we buried where he fell.

The four machine guns were set up at the four corners of our defence works, and protected as best they could be by hastily thrown up ramparts of sand. The men armed with rifles were distributed at equal distances along our fortifications. In the spaces between, were stationed the men who were armed with pistols only, and the ammunition was placed within easy reach. Our preparations were hardly completed when the men bringing the enemy's conditions, returned. The demands were that we surrender all arms and ammunition, our camels, all our provisions and water. In addition we were to pay eleven thousand pounds in gold. Upon compliance with these conditions we were to be allowed to proceed unmolested. Well we might!

The parleying had at first been conducted through the dragoman who, with his wife, had joined us at Coonfidah. He also was among the wounded. Shot in the leg! When he went over to the enemy to negotiate, he did not forget to take his wife with him. We did not see either of them again until we met them in Djidda.

My answer ran:

> In the first place, we have no money; in the second, we are guests of the country—get your money in Djidda; thirdly, it is not customary with Germans to surrender their arms.

Hereupon the firing began again. All the camel drivers who had so far remained with us, and a number of the Arab *gendarmes* also, took advantage of the truce to follow the example of the *dragoman* and his wife, and disappear. The engagement lasted until darkness came on. We lay very well protected behind our camel saddles and camels. We returned the enemy's fire but sparingly, as our store of ammunition was not large. Moreover, much of the ammunition that had gone down with the wrecked *zambuk*, and had lain in the water until we fished it out on the following morning, now missed fire. For this reason, I had all the undamaged ammunition placed in readiness near the machine guns, so that in a possible night attack at close range, I might feel sure of my most effective weapons.

The rest of the ammunition was distributed among the rifles. We suffered no further losses during the day's engagement. Several of our camels were shot, but we were none the less protected for this, as a dead camel is quite as good a shield against rifle balls as is a live one. We had eaten nothing during the entire day. Nor could we think of doing so while the daylight lasted. No sooner did one of us raise his head above our rampart of saddles, than the enemy's fire was redoubled.

But our most strenuous work began with the coming of the night. The moon did not rise until about an hour after sunset. During the intervening hour the darkness was so intense that we could see hardly forty or fifty metres ahead. Within our rampart everything was in readiness to withstand a night attack by storm. All rifles and pistols were loaded, the machine guns manned and ready for action, and the men, with their weapons in hand, were kneeling just behind the rampart. But nothing happened.

As soon as the moon had risen, and we could see as much as three hundred metres ahead, we set to work to improve our position. First of all, water was served to the men, and hard tack distributed. While some of the officers and men remained on guard ready for action, others set to work at deepening the trenches, an undertaking that proceeded but slowly, as we had no proper tools for the work. Still others were engaged in removing the dead camels from within our enclosure. The intense heat caused putrefaction to set in very rapidly. The carcasses swelled up, the tense hides burst, and the entrails exuded. As at this season of the year the wind blows persistently from the north, we took the dead camels to the southward of us, so that the stench might not sicken us.

It was well into the night before we felt free to take a little rest. The trenches were now so deep that they afforded ample shelter for the men lying in them. We had thrown up mounds of sand on all sides, in addition to the protection afforded us by the camels. Our rifles and pistols had suffered considerably from the incessantly drifting sand. They were now taken apart, a few at a time, cleaned and tested. Then we wrapped our handkerchiefs around the locks, and stuffed small bits of cloth into the muzzles to keep out the sand. All this care was necessary to insure the efficiency of our weapons. That there might always be someone on guard within our fortification, a part of the men remained awake at their posts while the others slept with their loaded rifles in their arms. There was always one officer awake. But nothing of importance occurred during the night.

At nine o'clock that evening, Lieutenant Schmidt, the officer who had been so terribly wounded, died. We dug a grave for him as deep as possible in the middle of our camping place, and toward eleven o'clock in the night, we four surviving officers ourselves bore our fallen comrade to his grave. There could be no service at the burial. The volley over his freshly made grave was fired by the enemy on the coming morning.

I had brought with me from Hodeida an English-speaking Arab. During the course of the night, as soon as the moon had risen, I sent this man to Djidda, only a ten hours' march by camel distant from us, and only eight by foot. I had found him to be a very reliable and sensible man, and, as I learned later, he succeeded in making his way through the enemy's lines, and took the report of our perilous situation to the military authorities at Djidda.

Half an hour before sunrise I had all hands roused. If the enemy had remained, there would, in all likelihood, be an attack made upon us as soon as the day had fully come. For the sake of the moral effect, it was my purpose to return their first fire with as heavy volleys as possible. I wished to convince the enemy that we were fully prepared for an attack, and that our fighting strength was undiminished.

What I had expected, happened. As the sun rose, our opponents opened a lively fire upon us. We gave them a vigorous answer with full volleys, and every head that showed itself received its share. This method of procedure perceptibly dampened the fighting spirit of our opponents. Their fire became noticeably weaker and more cautious. Our purpose was achieved.

just before sunrise all hands were served with a drink of water. During the entire course of the day there was not another opportunity to give them more. Not until after the sun had set could another drink be given them. As we did not find it possible to cook anything even at night, our store of hard tack was drawn upon, and every man stuffed his pockets full.

The enemy fired upon us without intermission. But, as we were pretty well protected, we returned their fire sparingly. That we were not engaged in an ordinary encounter with robbers, but were facing a thoroughly organized attack, now became doubly evident. From our fortified camp we could plainly see two large *zambuks* lying at anchor near the shore in the far distance. Between them and the Arabs who were besieging us, a regular relief system was being carried on. A large number of our foes must have come in these two ships. Others had arrived by land, which was shown by the fact that far off in the desert, near the horizon, a large number of camels could be seen grazing.

On this day, unhappily, two more of our men were severely wounded. Of these, Lanig, a fireman, was shot through the breast and abdomen, and died during the night. Unfortunately, we could give our wounded but little aid, as all our medical stores were lost together with the *zambuk* that foundered. All that we had left was the emergency bandage packages that we had brought with us from the *Emden*, and a few bottles of brandy.

The day brought forth nothing of special interest. A camel that had escaped from our enclosure was shot by a stray bullet to leeward of us, and the intense odour of decay that the wind brought with it was a source of annoyance. Within our camp itself, some very unpleasant guests had made their appearance. Hundreds and thousands of nasty black beetles about the length of a man's thumb ran about everywhere, carrying the camel dung all over the camp. Our trenches were alive with these insects, and it mattered little how many we killed, for new ones came to fill their places as fast as we killed them. Sleep was impossible. They crawled into our clothing, and ran over our faces. Aside from the annoyance they caused us, they brought a very real danger to our wounded. The *tetanus bacilli* develop more readily in horse and camel manure than in anything else, and the inevitable result of this infection is the deadly lockjaw.

The burning heat of the sun made life intolerable during the day. While firing, we could not wear our light-coloured head-cloths, as they afforded the enemy too good a target. The intense bright light dazzled our eyes, and made our heads ache. Everything was so hot that we burned our hands when, in firing, they occasionally touched the barrel of our rifles. The grease-soaked camel saddles began to smoulder in the heat, and a faint odour of smoke pervaded the whole camp. We got rid of this annoyance, as best we could, by heaping sand upon the saddles. The sand, carried by the never-ceasing wind, drifted over us incessantly. All day long some of us were kept busy digging out the trenches that had been half refilled with the drifting sand. It crept into our eyes, our ears, our mouths, and our noses. Our eyes became inflamed from its constant irritation. Dampened by sweat, it formed a thick coating on our faces by which they were disfigured beyond recognition. High in the air, just over our camp, circled from twenty to thirty great vultures.

With the approach of darkness everything within our camp was put into a state of preparedness again. And again I sent a message to

Djidda,—this time by two Arab *gendarmes* disguised as Bedouins. As soon as the moon had risen, those of us who were off duty lay down to rest. The enemy ceased firing as it grew dark.

In the middle of the night we were suddenly wakened by shots fired by some of our sentinels. In a twinkling everyone was at his post, ready to repel the supposed attack. "Where are they?" I asked one of the sentries.

"Right here, at a distance of about forty metres some of them were creeping along. There goes one now!" And off sped another bullet. But our supposed enemies were only hyenas and jackals, which, scenting prey, were sneaking about the camp, and making a meal of the dead camels.

When that night was ended, the sun rose over the horizon for the third time since the beginning of the fight. Our condition was critical. We had heard nothing from the Turkish garrison although, provided my messages had been received, relief might have reached us in the course of the preceding day. We could hold out no longer than to the end of this one day. By that time our supply of water would be exhausted, although each man had been allowed but one small cup full each morning and evening. Without water we were doomed. Whatever final action I decided upon, must therefore be undertaken at once, before my men had lost their strength. On that morning, I gave them orders to force their way through to Djidda as soon as the sun had set, if no relief reached us during the day. In this way I hoped that at least some of us would get there. Whoever fell, must fall. The sick and the wounded could not be taken with us. But it was not to come to that, thank God!

Toward noon of the third day a man waving a white cloth was seen coming over to us from the enemy, who had ceased firing. I had him brought within our camp, and asked him what he wanted. He replied that the other side would withdraw the demand for our arms, ammunition, camels, provisions, and water, if, instead, we would pay them twenty-two thousand pounds in gold. I conjectured that our foes had learned of the approach of the Turkish garrison, and that, in the customary way of the country, they were trying to get out of us what they could.

I determined to draw out the interview as long as possible, in the hope that the relief expected would arrive in the meantime, and the enemy would then be caught between two fires. For this reason I pictured our situation in as rosy a light as possible, and as though we could wish for nothing better than to spend a summer vacation in the desert, entertained by the music of whistling bullets about us. I pointed to our empty water cans where they lay buried in the sand, and gave the man to understand that we had water enough to last us four weeks easily, that there was therefore no reason why I should make special concessions, and furthermore, that we had an abundance of ammunition, as he himself had reason to know.

In fact the enemy ought to be thankful that I had not come down upon them with my machine guns. The medium of our conversation was a native of Morocco, a man who, at some former time, had been made prisoner of war in Belgium, and, together with a number of other Mohammedans, had been sent back to Turkey. From there he had joined an expedition to Arabia, and had come to Coonfidah, where I ran across him and took him with us. He understood a few words of French.

The enemy's envoy did not seem especially elated by my representations. He withdrew, only to return again in about half an hour with a repetition of the selfsame terms. To gain time, I now told him that I considered it highly important that I should confer with the leader of our assailants in person, and I therefore besought him to come to me, here in my camp. His apprehensive Highness did not come, but sent, instead, the fierce threat that if we did not pay at once, we should have "*beaucoup de combat*." I interpreted this to mean that for him it was high time to get his train. So I expressed my surprise that he did not regard what had occurred as "*beaucoup de combat*." To me it had seemed to be such, I said.

Hereupon there blazed out from the enemy's lines a few more furiously angry volleys, and then silence fell.

A quarter of an hour passed, and then another, and not a shot was heard. Slowly and cautiously we raised our heads above our camel saddle ramparts. Nothing to be seen!

Careful," I cautioned. "This is only a ruse. Keep down! There is time enough. We can't get away from here before evening in any case."

But when nothing at all happened, we first got up on our knees, then on our feet, and then searched all about with our glasses. Nothing to be seen! Whither our foes had vanished, we had not the least idea. The sand hills of the desert, into which they had gone, concealed them from our view. Apparently they had departed.

For the present I meant under any circumstances to remain where we were. In the first place, I did not feel at all certain that the enemy had really withdrawn, and that this was not merely a ruse to which they had resorted. And secondly, we could not take up our march before nightfall in any case.

About an hour after the firing had ceased, two men on camels appeared in the distance. Their dress and richly caparisoned saddles proclaimed them from afar to be no ordinary Bedouins. Waving a white cloth, they came riding toward our camp. As a sign that we understood their purpose, we raised our war flag. When the men had come to within fifty metres of us, they dismounted. I sent my man from Morocco out to them, to ask what they wanted. The answer was that they wished to speak with the commander of the German troop. They had been sent by the *Emir* of Mecca, who had been informed of the attack upon us, and was sending troops to our relief.

This sounded very promising, but there was after all no surety that it was really true. By this time my sojourn in Arabia had taught me to be suspicious of everything. When I went out to meet the Arabs, it was with drawn sword in hand, and behind me walked one of my men with cocked rifle, ready to shoot. At the camp I left orders to stand ready to fire, and, in case an attack upon me should be made, to shoot without regard for my person. But again nothing happened.

The two Arabs assured me that Abdullah, the second son of the *Emir* of Mecca, would soon arrive with a company of soldiers. And truly, in about another half hour we could see in the distance about seventy men riding toward us on camels, and carrying before them a dark red banner emblazoned with verses from the Koran in golden lettering. They were making a sort of music by the beating of drums, and were singing to it. I regarded this proceeding as rather incautious, if, as I assumed, these soldiers were about to enter into an engagement.

Coming toward me, Abdullah saluted. He brought me his father's greetings, and expressed regret for what had occurred. He told me that he had brought us water, and assured me that we could now march on to Djidda in peace, as our assailants had withdrawn.

After I had distributed the water among my men, we proceeded to load the packs on the camels. This was a wearisome undertaking, and one that was accompanied by many difficulties, as getting camels ready to march has as yet not been included in the training for service in the Imperial navy. Quantities of provisions had to be left behind, as forty of our camels had been shot.

Accompanied by the *emir's* troops we left our camp. It was, no doubt, a most unusual occurrence that a Christian should thus be riding through the desert, side by side with the son of the *Emir* of Mecca, and under the banner of the Prophet. A few minutes later we passed the abandoned positions of our foes. The rascals had actually dug out regular trenches for themselves.

We rode throughout the rest of the day. In the evening we camped beside a spring. Here, for the first time in four days, we could eat a cooked meal, wash ourselves, and lie down to rest. A circumstance of interest was that the water was brought up from a well having a depth of about forty metres, and yet its temperature was about thirty degrees Centigrade.[1]

As we lay in our camp, close by the shore of the sea, we could see, in the darkness of the night, the restless play of a searchlight flashing over the surface of the water. Our friends, the Englishmen off Djidda!

1. A depth of about 131 feet, and a temperature of 86 degrees Fahrenheit.—Translator.

Chapter 13

To the Railroad

We were well cared for at Djidda. The sick and wounded found shelter and attention in a comparatively good military hospital. A difficult point for me to settle now, was how it was best to proceed on our way. I had learned that the Bedouins who had attacked us were in the service of the English, a fact to which the modern English rifles with which they were equipped, attested. The way out of Djidda by sea was also closed to us. During the day we could distinctly see the mast tops of the English blockaders now and again. Nevertheless, I decided to continue our journey in *zambuks*. It appeared to me that the way by water offered greater possibilities of success than to travel by land.

The first step to be taken was to spread abroad the report that we intended to go overland. Meanwhile, very secretly, I provided myself with a *zambuk* and a good pilot. On account of the wounded it was necessary to remain in Djidda for some days. The eighth of April was the day set for our departure. In the harbour at Djidda there was a motorboat in which I made a trip of inspection as far out to sea as possible. I saw no sign of the English. Did they believe in the rumoured land journey?

On the night between the eighth and ninth of April the wind was in our favour, and we ran out. We met much better conditions than when we ran the English blockade upon leaving Hodeida. The wind held steady all through the night, and when the sun rose, we were out of sight of the blockading Englishmen. I hugged the shore with my *zambuk* as well as I could, and took advantage of every reef to creep behind it, and so increase the difficulty of our capture by any possible pursuers. Our progress was slow but sure. We stopped for a short time, generally not more than a few hours, at several little coast towns to inquire for news, and to purchase fresh provisions.

The pilot we had taken with us from Djidda was thoroughly familiar with the waters through which he was conducting us, and spoke English very well. We lay at anchor at night, as the reefs rendered navigation impossible in the dark. At Sherm Rabigh I had to change *zambuks*, as the one I had procured at Djidda proved to be too weak. Our new *zambuk* had first of all to be ballasted with sand, as, without either cargo or ballast, the ship could not carry sail.

Our anchoring, in the evening, was always a peculiar manoeuvre. In the proper sense of the word anchoring, it was not such at all. The coral reefs between which we were sailing fell off abruptly all round into a great depth of water. The anchoring proceeded in this way: We ran to within a few metres of the coral reefs, where we took down all sails. Two Arabs, standing ready at the bow, then jumped overboard, each one carrying with him a light rope to which iron hooks were attached. These iron hooks were bored into the cavities of the coral formation just below the surface of the water. And so we lay for the night. This was not always pleasant however, for when the wind shifted, there was danger that it would blow us onto the coral formation to which we had made fast.

On our way to the north we passed several boats sailing in the opposite direction. It is the custom in Arabia for boatmen, in passing, to greet each other with a sort of howl. The Arabs in the boats we met were always amazed to hear, as they sailed by us, the howling of their countrymen in our *zambuk* energetically supplemented by fifty vigorous voices.

We found practically no coast population along the entire way, but occasionally we met, far out at sea, a little dugout carrying an Arab or two engaged in fishing. We always hailed these fishermen, and traded rice for fish with them.

Our way northward took us past Mecca. It is the custom with Arabs, when at their prayers five times a day, to face toward their Holy City, and to touch their foreheads to the ground in that direction. So it came about that during the first days of our sailing, the Arabs in our *zambuk* would stand facing toward the bows, then, later, to starboard, and finally they faced aft.

Without meeting with any special difficulties we reached Sherm Munnaiburra on the twenty-eighth day of April. This is a little sheltered bay about ten nautical miles south of our intended point of destination, El Wegh. From this bay onward our course lay without the shelter of the reefs, and deep water ran close to the shore. We had now been fighting our way onward for nearly six months, and there prevailed among us a general disinclination to trust ourselves to a sail-boat over this last short stretch that might prove dangerous to us on our journey. For this reason we cast anchor at Sherm Munnaiburra, to go overland to El Wegh.

Our coming had been made known to the local authorities by messengers despatched overland, who had arrived before us. A few *gendarmes* had therefore been sent to the coast to meet us. We got hold of one of them while we were still in the harbour, and sent him out to find camels for us. Before the night had passed, we could see from where we lay, a number of little watch fires burning here and there along the shore, an indication that the animals for our caravan were assembling.

When we rode off on the following day, we took with us nothing more than our arms, and provisions sufficient for one day only. Everything else was left on the *zambuk*, to take its chances by sea. Fortunately, the *zambuk* reached its destination without sighting a single hostile ship. On the evening of the twenty-ninth day of April we were in El Wegh.

The first thing we did here was to get a good bath, and a good sleep. Here, too, we at last had an opportunity to change our underclothing and have it washed, for it required two days to get the necessary camels together at El Wegh.

On the second of May, at eight o'clock in the morning, we began our march. Here in the north, the camels travelled differently than in the south, where, as has been described, they were all tied together so as to form one long line. This is not the custom in the north, where every animal goes along by itself, and must be guided by its own rider. At first this proved a difficult task for my men, but before long they had their camels so well in hand that the caravan could be kept together quite well. We were conducted on our way by Suleiman, Sheikh of El Wegh.

At first our road lay through the desert with which we were all too familiar. But very soon we came to a mountain region, and passed some charming scenery. The water conditions also were far better than those we had found in the desert. The wells were better kept, and furnished water that was at least drinkable, although not absolutely clean. That we should see running water when we reached the mountain ridge was announced to us by our Arab escort, days before we got there, as a matter of special interest and wonder. If any of us were anticipating the pleasure of bathing in a mountain torrent, our hopes were certainly doomed to disappointment. To be sure, the water in the tiny rivulet that we saw did move, but any one of us could easily have stopped its flow for some time, by stepping into it with both feet.

Up here in the mountains, where it was cooler, we marched by day, and rested at night. Because of our bitter experience in the desert, we made it our habit to intrench ourselves every evening before going to sleep, much to the astonishment of our Arab escort. But we had finally reached the point where we doubted that anybody was to be trusted. Our fortifications were usually very quickly thrown up, as we had brought with us spades enough for all. And so, each evening saw a small fortified camp arise in the wilderness, and from out its ramparts our four machine guns protruded threateningly. Within our fortifications no watch fire was allowed, but the immediate region all round our camp was well lighted by fires kept burning by our sentinels. We slept, as usual, with loaded rifles in our arms. Comfort was not a prominent feature in this sort of camp. The nights were very cold. The well men among us frequently gave their blankets to the sick, that they might be kept warm. But those of us who had none did not mind it, but followed the old rule which runs: "*Lie down on your back and cover yourself with your belly.*"

The domain of our conductor, Suleiman Pasha, did not extend quite to El Ula, from whence we expected to go by the Hejaz Railroad. just before reaching El Ula we had to cross territory that was controlled by another sheikh, one who was at enmity with our friend, and who was illy disposed toward us because we had not hired camels of him for the last four hours of our march, while passing through his territory.

Under these circumstances it was quite possible that we still might have to break our way through by force of arms. Suleiman Pasha also seemed to regard something of this kind as probable. On each day, and from every direction in the mountains, small bands of his adherents joined him, until our caravan had gradually attained a total strength of some four hundred men. It was a most picturesque scene we looked upon as these Bedouins marched along, carrying long Arab flintlocks, clad in their loosely flowing brown garments, and with fluttering bright bead-cloths. If, on the preceding days, we had been the only ones to be cautious enough to intrench, it was now Suleiman Pasha himself who adopted this measure, an evidence to us that it might yet be made pretty hot for us. That night we made special efforts to be well prepared. But it passed without disturbance of any kind.

We were now only one day's journey distant from a railroad station. Our way lay over a high mountain region. We wound along through narrow passes that seemed just fitted for an attack. Through these defiles but one camel could pass at a time, with the result, that the caravan stretched away in so long a line that it could hardly be kept together under the command of one leader. To guard against any possible surprise, Suleiman had organized a regular reconnoitring service, which, in its wonderful efficiency, was worthy of admiration. Perhaps it was also an evidence that he had frequent need of it. Little patrols, mounted on camels, rushed at a full gallop into every mountain valley, emerged on the other side of the mountain, made their observations, reported, and returned to their places in the caravan.

When we were but a few hours' march distant from El Ula, letters were brought to us. They had been sent to inform us that the angry sheikh who, we had supposed, would attack us, was at the time embroiled in a fight farther to the north, and that we could therefore continue on our way without fear of being molested.

Upon receipt of this information I decided to ride ahead of the caravan, so as to get to the telegraph station at El Ula as soon as possible, order a special train, and make arrangements for the comfort of my men. I was accompanied by Suleiman Pasha, his two sons, and several other dignitaries. We rode at a sharp trot, and covered the last stretch of the journey in a few hours. We had all come to be on very friendly terms with our Sheikh and his two sons, although our means of conversation were very limited.

All three of them showed the greatest interest when, on arriving at the summit of the mountain range, from whence the white houses of El Ula could be seen gleaming out from among the palm trees, I took out my binoculars to get sight at last of a telegraph wire and a railroad. Glasses of this kind are as yet unknown in this region. Each of my Arab friends wanted to get at least one look through them, and so the glasses passed from hand to hand. With every change of hands, the glasses were given an extra turn. How much the last one could see, I cannot say.

In order to impress our Arab escort at the very outset with the efficiency of our weapons, I had, some days previously, given Suleiman Pasha, to his great astonishment, an illustration of what our machine guns were capable of in the way of firing. He was eager to be allowed himself to press the button, and manifested a surprised delight when the gun, which we had got ready for him beforehand, fired an unbroken succession of shots, and brought down pieces of stone from the cliffs at which it was aimed. As all weapons are subjects of great interest to Arabs, I presented Suleiman Pasha and each of his sons with a revolver and the necessary ammunition for it. In addition, I promised to send them a binocular from Germany.

As we were riding across a wide plateau which stretched beyond the limits of our vision, I utilized this opportunity to impress upon the Pasha an idea of Germany's greatness. To his amazement he was told that German warships, when engaged in battle, could fire upon the enemy from a distance considerably greater than the breadth of the plain we were then traversing. Although this was a slight exaggeration, for the tableland stretched from horizon to horizon, it produced the desired effect. The size of the guns from which these shots were fired, I pictured to him by saying that a sheep could easily run through the barrel of any one of them.

Toward noon we arrived at El Ula, and, much to my surprise, everything was in readiness for us. A special train stood waiting for us, its engine all ready for the order to light the fires. This order was not long delayed.

Two German gentlemen and a number of Turkish officers had come to meet us; letters and news from the colonies in Syria were awaiting us. We were treated to chilled Rhine wine, champagne, peaches, and other delicacies of which we had long been deprived. Being given the choice between a glass of wine and a bath, I chose the former. Why depart so suddenly from a familiar habit to which one had faithfully adhered for weeks past?

A few hours later my men arrived. I rode out a short distance to meet them. With flag flying, and cameras pointed at us from every side, we marched together into the little town where a railroad and a waiting room gave us the first indication that we were returning to civilization. An abundant meal, a greater abundance to drink, and a quick bath (after all!) occupied the next few hours. Then the train moved northward at the wonderful speed of thirty kilometres an hour, and we could yield our weary limbs to the comfort of red-cushioned seats, a luxury long denied us.

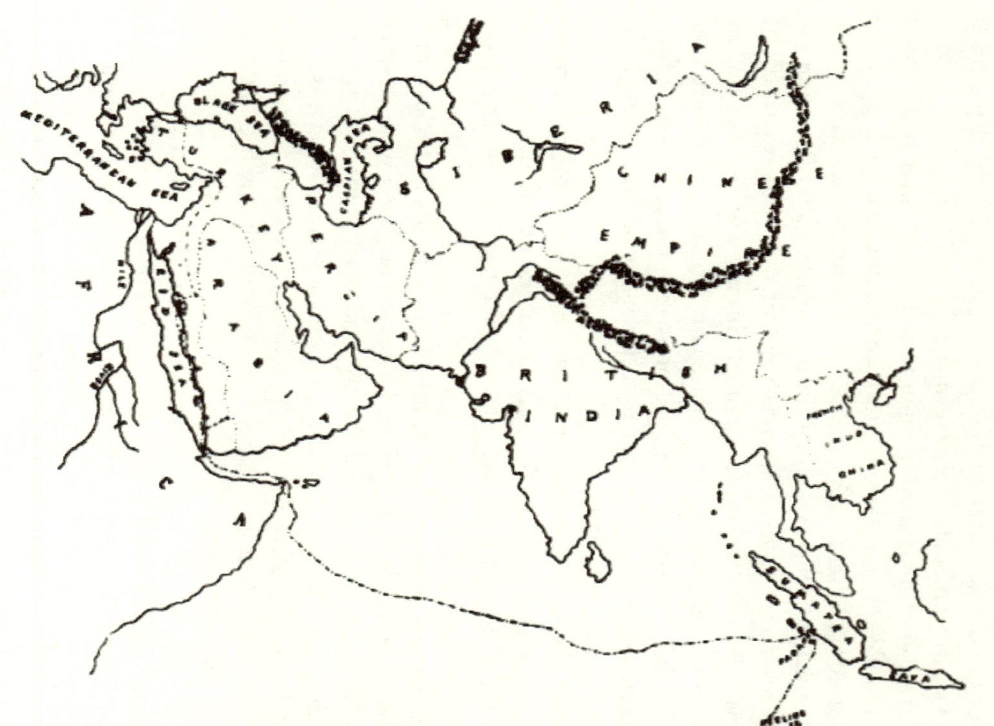

— — — — — This line marks the approximate course of the journey traveled by Lieut. von Mücke and his men.

Chapter 14

Homeward Bound

Henceforth our journey was free from danger of any kind. We travelled by rail over Damascus and Aleppo through Asia Minor to Constantinople. At two points on our journey we had to leave the railroad and travel by wagon, or afoot, as the railroad had not been completed at these places.

Everywhere we were entertained most cordially and hospitably by our German countrymen and by the Turkish authorities. At the railway stations large crowds were always assembled to greet us. There were bands playing and flags flying to welcome us, and roses with which to decorate ourselves. Gifts were showered upon us as we sat in our carriages. New clothing was provided for us, and we shed no tears when we parted from our old rags and their numerous inhabitants.

My men enjoyed the unprecedented distinction of dining with great dignitaries and men high in authority. Costly presents were bestowed upon us, and our baggage car, that at one time had held nothing but rags and our munitions, now filled up more and more. At some of the way stations at which our train stopped only on our account, large numbers of Bedouins had gathered to see us. They raced along beside our train, and when it stopped, they gave us an exhibition of fancy riding. Many a social glass was drained in the company of our German compatriots.

At last, in Aleppo, we received news from home, the first in ten months. Letters from loved ones and the Iron Cross! What more could the heart desire? There were two large mail bags full, and we devoted the next few days to our mail from home, to reading the many letters and verses that had been sent us, to writing autographs, and to making away with the cigars, chocolates, and other good things that had been given us.

During the afternoon of Whitsunday our train pulled into the station at Haider Pasha, the Asiatic terminus of the railway. Here my men received their long-wished-for German uniforms, which had been forwarded to them. The officers also had succeeded in procuring for themselves an outfit conforming, in a measure at least, to the demands made by the European civilization to which we were returning.

The chief of our Mediterranean Division, who was also chief of the Turkish fleet, Admiral Souchon, had honoured us by coming with his staff to meet us at Haider Pasha. My men quickly fell in line. Our flag, which we had followed for ten months, was flying at our right wing. A few brief commands, the execution of which proved that the brigand existence we had led for months had not destroyed our military trim, and my sword was lowered before my superior officer:

"I report the landing squad from the *Emden*, five officers, seven petty officers, and thirty men strong."

ALSO FROM LEONAUR

AVAILABLE IN SOFTCOVER OR HARDCOVER WITH DUST JACKET

BOOTS AND SADDLES *by Elizabeth B. Custer*—The experiences of General Custer's Wife on the Western Plains.

FANNIE BEERS' CIVIL WAR *by Fannie A. Beers*—A Confederate Lady's Experiences of Nursing During the Campaigns & Battles of the American Civil War.

LADY SALE'S AFGHANISTAN *by Florentia Sale*—An Indomitable Victorian Lady's Account of the Retreat from Kabul During the First Afghan War.

THE TWO WARS OF MRS DUBERLY *by Frances Isabella Duberly*—An Intrepid Victorian Lady's Experience of the Crimea and Indian Mutiny.

LADIES OF WATERLOO *by Charlotte A. Eaton, Magdalene de Lancey & Juana Smith*—The Experiences of Three Women During the Campaign of 1815: Waterloo Days by Charlotte A. Eaton, A Week at Waterloo by Magdalene de Lancey & Juana's Story by Juana Smith.

DESPATCH RIDER *by W. H. L. Watson*—The Experiences of a British Army Motorcycle Despatch Rider During the Opening Battles of the Great War in Europe.

TWO YEARS BEFORE THE MAST *by Richard Henry Dana. Jr.*—The account of one young man's experiences serving on board a sailing brig—the Penelope—bound for California, between the years1834-36.

A SAILOR OF KING GEORGE *by Frederick Hoffman*—From Midshipman to Captain—Recollections of War at Sea in the Napoleonic Age 1793-1815.

LORDS OF THE SEA *by A. T. Mahan*—Great Captains of the Royal Navy During the Age of Sail.

COGGESHALL'S VOYAGES: VOLUME 1 *by George Coggeshall*—The Recollections of an American Schooner Captain.

COGGESHALL'S VOYAGES: VOLUME 2 *by George Coggeshall*—The Recollections of an American Schooner Captain.

TWILIGHT OF EMPIRE *by Sir Thomas Ussher & Sir George Cockburn*—Two accounts of Napoleon's Journeys in Exile to Elba and St. Helena: Narrative of Events by Sir Thomas Ussher & Napoleon's Last Voyage: Extract of a diary by Sir George Cockburn.

KIEL AND JUTLAND *by Georg Von Hase*—The Famous Naval Battle of the First World War from the German Perspective.

ALSO FROM LEONAUR

AVAILABLE IN SOFTCOVER OR HARDCOVER WITH DUST JACKET

ESCAPE FROM THE FRENCH *by Edward Boys*—A Young Royal Navy Midshipman's Adventures During the Napoleonic War.

THE VOYAGE OF H.M.S. PANDORA *by Edward Edwards R. N. & George Hamilton, edited by Basil Thomson*—In Pursuit of the Mutineers of the Bounty in the South Seas—1790-1791.

MEDUSA *by J. B. Henry Savigny and Alexander Correard and Charlotte-Adélaïde Dard* —Narrative of a Voyage to Senegal in 1816 & The Sufferings of the Picard Family After the Shipwreck of the Medusa.

THE SEA WAR OF 1812 VOLUME 1 *by A. T. Mahan*—A History of the Maritime Conflict.

THE SEA WAR OF 1812 VOLUME 2 *by A. T. Mahan*—A History of the Maritime Conflict.

WETHERELL OF H. M. S. HUSSAR *by John Wetherell*—The Recollections of an Ordinary Seaman of the Royal Navy During the Napoleonic Wars.

THE NAVAL BRIGADE IN NATAL *by C. R. N. Burne*—With the Guns of H. M. S. Terrible & H. M. S. Tartar during the Boer War 1899-1900.

THE VOYAGE OF H. M. S. BOUNTY *by William Bligh*—The True Story of an 18th Century Voyage of Exploration and Mutiny.

SHIPWRECK! *by William Gilly*—The Royal Navy's Disasters at Sea 1793-1849.

KING'S CUTTERS AND SMUGGLERS: 1700-1855 *by E. Keble Chatterton*—A unique period of maritime history-from the beginning of the eighteenth to the middle of the nineteenth century when British seamen risked all to smuggle valuable goods from wool to tea and spirits from and to the Continent.

CONFEDERATE BLOCKADE RUNNER *by John Wilkinson*—The Personal Recollections of an Officer of the Confederate Navy.

NAVAL BATTLES OF THE NAPOLEONIC WARS *by W. H. Fitchett*—Cape St. Vincent, the Nile, Cadiz, Copenhagen, Trafalgar & Others.

PRISONERS OF THE RED DESERT *by R. S. Gwatkin-Williams*—The Adventures of the Crew of the Tara During the First World War.

U-BOAT WAR 1914-1918 *by James B. Connolly/Karl von Schenk*—Two Contrasting Accounts from Both Sides of the Conflict at Sea D uring the Great War.

www.ingramcontent.com/pod-product-compliance
Lightning Source LLC
LaVergne TN
LVHW091640100826
845152LV00006B/112/J

* 9 7 8 0 8 5 7 0 6 8 4 2 2 *